STANDARD GRADE
Administration
course notes

Text Copyright © 2002 (2nd Edition) Ed Milne and Janice Milne
Illustrations © 2000 Leckie & Leckie Ltd
Cover images © Jack Hollingsworth/Brand X Pictures and Ingram Publishing

Published by
Leckie & Leckie Ltd
8 Whitehill Terrace
St Andrews KY16 8RN
Scotland
tel: 01334 475656
fax: 01334 477392
e-mail: enquiries@leckieandleckie.co.uk
web: www.leckieandleckie.co.uk

Edited by
Helen Webster

Special thanks to
Caleb Rutherford (cover design)

ISBN 1-898890-96-X

A CIP Catalogue record for this book is available from the British Library.

Leckie & Leckie Ltd is a division of Granada Learning Limited, part of ITV plc.

Ed Milne ✕ Janice Milne

Contents

Acknowledgement

The screenshots of Microsoft products on pages 37, 67 and 69 are reprinted with permission from Microsoft Corporation. Leckie & Leckie also acknowledges Microsoft Corporation's trademarks, as well as any other trademarks mentioned in this book.

Disclaimer

The names, addresses and other details of the following people, companies and products are fictitious and are used for illustrative purposes only: Sam Ryan (pages 4, 6, 7, 9, 27, 28, 40, 46, 47, 59, 68 and 78); Made4IT (pages 4, 5, 6, 10 ,11, 14, 15, 16, 17, 23, 27, 28, 31, 39, 40, 41, 42, 46, 47, 53, 68, 71, 73, 77, 78 and 80); British Association of Office Designers (page 5); Perth Daily Echo (page 10); Katie Blair and York Universal Supplies (pages 21, 46 and 47); Wheaty Flakes (page 22); Pauline Stuart (page 27); Jenny Kerr (pages 28 and 40); Gerry McQuade, James Dignan, Ruth Chalmers, Margaret Joyce, Paul Johnson and Duncan Simpson (page 28); Bhar Karim and Fast Forward Ltd (pages 37, 54 and 55); Mr Fairgrieve and Quentin Designs (page 40); C Thompson, W Patterson, R McKay, T Clements, P Noble, Craigmore plc, P Bruce, Sinclair Graphics, R Cooke, J Akhtar, ART Design,S Steven, T Lindsay, Hitchens Ltd, S Parish, KL Photographers, C Izatt and A Ridland (page 41); Bloggs & Sons (page 42); S Dexter, Cleo's Restaurant, Clean-It-Up, Blackett PLC, Baldwin & Sons, K Baker, Andorra & Co Ltd, Agate Car Hire and D Abott (page 51); Arts and Media, Dundee Security Ltd, David Moffat & Sons, Brown Brothers, Border PC Services, The Wedding Shop, PG Computers plc, De Luxe Printers, P & J Insurance Co, Struan Windows, Eskbank Design Co, Mike Copland, Rosie Hakim, Laura Gregor, Katie Foley, Nicholas Briggs, Elizabeth Nauman, Ellie Snowdon, Ian Johnson, Kate Archibald, Miles Wylie, Lynette Brown (pages 54 and 55); Salespersons Anderson, Lee, Mackenzie, Morven, Peters (pages 55, 56 and 57); Salesperson Bathgate (pages 56 and 57); City Hotel (page 65); Steven Lewis (page 71); Nancy Wilson (pages 71 and 76); Karen Law, and Saunders and Kievel (page 73); Dean Office Services, Ryan Spence, Waterloo Hotel, Grand Hotel Martinn, Alain Hartelaub and Stephanie Merlo, Euro Designs (page 76); Graham Smith (pages 77 and 80); Star Travel Ltd and Hotel Opera (page 78); Scotiabank, Andy McTuffheid and Jock McTuffheid (page 79).

Introduction

Standard Grade Administration is usually a two-year course of study. There are two main Areas of Study:
1 Administrative Support
2 Information and Communications Technology (ICT).

Within the Areas of Study you will learn about the following:

Area of Study 1: Administrative Support

1 Introduction to Business Organisations (organisation of departments; key functions of departments within an organisation)
2 The Working Environment (office layout; safe working practices and procedures; reception services; mail handling)
3 Storage and Retrieval of Information (purpose of filing; methods; security of information)
4 Reprographics
5 Sources of Information (paper-based and electronic)
6 Preparation and Presentation of Information
7 Travel (arrangements; paying for travel)

Area of Study 2: Information and Communications Technology

1 Communications (voicemail, intranet, Internet, e-mail, fax, electronic diary, etc)
2 Databases
3 File Management
4 Spreadsheets
5 Word Processing

How is the Course Assessed?

The course is broken down into three assessable elements. A grade is awarded for each element and it is these grades which will be shown on your Scottish Qualifications Certificate. The assessable elements are:
• **Knowledge and Understanding**
• **Problem Solving**
• **Practical Abilities**.

Knowledge and Understanding and **Problem Solving** are externally assessed, ie you sit examinations which are set and marked by Scottish Qualifications Authority (SQA) examiners (usually teachers). You will sit the examination papers at a main diet of SQA examinations.

Practical Abilities is also externally assessed. Performance is based on a series of integrated tasks which are externally set and externally marked by the SQA.

What is the Purpose of these Course Notes?

These Course Notes are designed to assist you in preparing for the written examination papers which assess Knowledge and Understanding and Problem Solving. The questions within the examination papers will draw largely upon the content of Area of Study 1 (Administrative Support).

The Notes are set out as seven sections – these represent the syllabus sections within Area of Study 1 (Administrative Support). Aspects of Knowledge and Understanding and Problem Solving from Area of Study 2 (Information and Communications Technology) have been included at appropriate points in the Notes.

Are these Course Notes Useful for Intermediate 1 and Intermediate 2 Courses in Administration?

Yes. They cover a substantial part of the content of the Administrative Support Units.

Layout of the Course Notes

When the meaning of a word or phrase is being given it will be shown with an '=' sign. You do not have to learn each definition word for word but it is useful if you know what the word or phrase means.

There has been no attempt to separate Foundation level content from General level content. The content for Credit level has, however, been indicated with ⓒ→ to the left of the relevant sections. If you are sitting the Foundation and General level examinations, you may choose to ignore the Credit level content and concentrate on the content for Foundation and General levels only. If you are sitting the General and Credit level examinations then you will have to be familiar with all of the content of these Course Notes.

Setting the Scene

Sam Ryan is 20 years old. Sam is the Administration Supervisor in the Administration Department of Made4IT. You can see Sam's position in the organisation chart of Made4IT which is shown on page 6. Sam supervises the word processing, mailroom, reprographics and reception staff. Sam may be called upon to deputise for staff when they are on holiday or off work because they are ill.

Made4IT is a large company which designs office layouts and customises office furniture and fittings. The company's headquarters is in Perth. More information about the company is given in the promotional flyer which is shown on page 5.

At times within these Course Notes we shall refer to Sam and/or Made4IT to provide further examples of what is being described.

**10 Newhouse Avenue
PERTH
PHI2 6XJ**

Who are we?

We have been designing office layouts and customising office furniture and fittings for the past 20 years. In 1999 we were awarded the prestigious Gold Award of the British Association of Office Designers (BAOD) for outstanding performance in office design. This will be our platform for continued success in Y2K and beyond!

What do we do?

We are specialists in designing office layouts to accommodate the latest advances in Information and Communications Technology (ICT) – from stand-alone computer systems to those connected to local and wide area networks, intranets and the Internet.

Where are we?

From our headquarters in the beautiful city of Perth we service hundreds of organisations throughout the UK. We have depots in Belfast, Birmingham, Cardiff, Manchester, Newcastle and London which provide both a local service and ensure that our products are delivered to your door in the fastest possible time.

What can we do for you?

We can design your office of tomorrow to ensure that you take maximum advantage of developments in teleworking and hot desking. Whatever your needs, be it the traditional or the futuristic, we are here to offer quality advice and support to ensure that your systems are efficient and effective.

How can you contact us?

For an informal discussion of your needs, please don't hesitate to get in touch.

**tel: OI738 622656
fax: OI738 62266I
email: hq@made4it.co.uk
internet: www.made4it.co.uk**

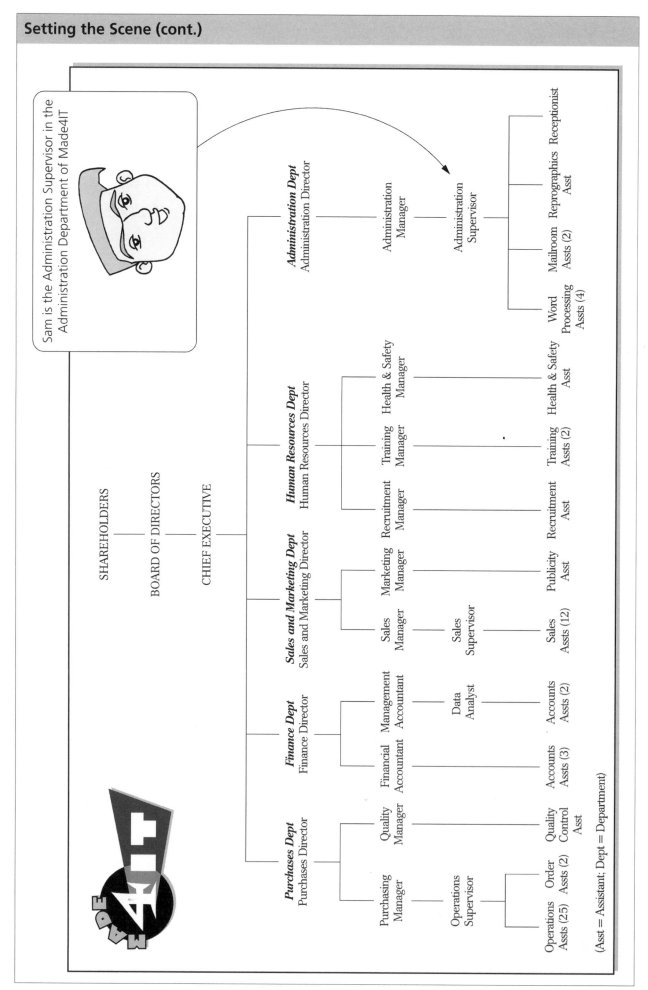

Sam is the Administration Supervisor in the Administration Department of Made4IT

SHAREHOLDERS

BOARD OF DIRECTORS

CHIEF EXECUTIVE

Purchases Dept
Purchases Director

Purchasing Manager — Quality Manager

Operations Supervisor

Operations Assts (25) — Order Assts (2) — Quality Control Asst

Finance Dept
Finance Director

Financial Accountant — Management Accountant

Data Analyst

Accounts Assts (3) — Accounts Assts (2)

Sales and Marketing Dept
Sales and Marketing Director

Sales Manager — Marketing Manager

Sales Supervisor

Sales Assts (12) — Publicity Asst

Human Resources Dept
Human Resources Director

Recruitment Manager — Training Manager — Health & Safety Manager

Recruitment Asst — Training Assts (2) — Health & Safety Asst

Administration Dept
Administration Director

Administration Manager

Administration Supervisor

Word Processing Assts (4) — Mailroom Assts (2) — Reprographics Asst — Receptionist

(Asst = Assistant; Dept = Department)

1a Introduction to Business Organisations: Organisation of Departments

What does an organisation chart show?

An organisation chart shows:
- the management structure and main departments within an organisation (Human Resources/Personnel, Finance, Purchases, Sales and Marketing, etc)
- the titles of main jobs (posts) within an organisation and within each department – organisation charts may also show the names of the people holding each of the main posts
- the relationship between the various posts – posts which have the same level of authority or responsibility are shown on the same level
- the reporting structure – a person will usually report to, and be accountable to, the person immediately above her/him on the organisation chart
- the number of people who are accountable to each manager.

An organisation chart will not usually show all of the jobs in an organisation – there simply isn't the space!

> **Organisation chart** = the management structure of an organisation shown as a diagram
>
> **Accountability** = the obligation an employee has to justify or explain her/his actions or decisions (an employee will be accountable to her/his line manager)
>
> **Authority** = the power that an employee has to instruct others and take decisions
>
> **Responsibility** = the obligation an employee has to carry out a range of tasks or duties (duties may include supervising other people)

An employee will usually report to the person(s) immediately above her/him on the organisation chart. If, for some reason, that person is not available then the employee will report to the next person further up the chart.

If the Admin Manager is not available, Sam reports to the Admin Director.

Employees who are on the same level within the same department will usually communicate with each other about their work. They will not usually be expected to communicate about their work with employees on the same level in other departments.

What are the benefits of preparing an organisation chart?

Customers or visitors to a firm:
- gain an immediate impression of the overall size of the organisation
- gain an immediate impression of the type of work carried out by the organisation
- are given a better idea of who to contact within the organisation.

Employees of a firm:
- can immediately see the overall size and structure of the organisation (how the various sections are grouped and the main areas of work of departments/sections)
- can see at a glance the reporting structures and lines of communication within the organisation
- can see the number of people who are accountable to each senior manager
- can immediately see the relationship of the departments and managers within the organisation
- are made aware of the range of activities undertaken by the organisation.

What is the usual shape of an organisation chart?

An organisation chart is usually shaped like a pyramid with a few senior or high status posts at the top of the pyramid, with a greater number of lower status posts at each of the levels below. In a **pyramid** (or **hierarchical**) **structure**, posts with the same level of authority/responsibility are shown on the same level.

There may be many levels of posts within an organisation. The pyramid structure of an organisation with seven levels of posts may appear as shown:

Chief Executive

Directors

Senior Managers

Managers

Junior Managers

Supervisors

Assistants

> **Pyramid (hierarchical) structure** = posts with the same status or authority are grouped together and shown on the same level – posts with more authority are shown above and those with less authority below

4 WP Assts, 2 Mailroom Assts, 1 Reprographics Asst, 1 Receptionist – I have 8 people in my span of control

The **span of control** of a manager refers to the number of staff who report directly to the manager. A manager with a wide span of control will have many staff reporting directly to her/him; a manager with a narrow span of control will have few staff reporting directly to her/him. Managers with wide spans of control have to be able to **delegate** work. Where the span of control is narrow it is easier for the manager to supervise and keep control of the work of her/his staff.

> **Span of control** = the number of staff reporting directly to a manager
>
> **Delegate** = pass on to selected employees the authority and responsibility to carry out a task or activity

A pyramid structure with many levels of posts is known as a tall structure. In recent years there has been a move towards removing certain levels of management posts (known as delayering). This has resulted in flatter structures. Delayering an organisation will lead to more posts at each of the remaining levels.

> **Tall management structure** = a structure which has many levels of management posts
>
> **Flat management structure** = a structure which has few levels of management posts

Why do organisations use teams?

Organisations often use teams to come up with solutions to problems or to improve the quality of the organisation's products/services.

Features of effective teams:
- everyone shares a common goal or sense of purpose
- everyone in the team is committed to achieving the goal
- there is team planning and discussion of tactics
- members of the team are committed to doing their best for the team
- members help each other – they encourage and praise one another
- every team member takes responsibility for the success or lack of success of the team
- the team makes best use of the skills, experience and expertise of each team member

What are the advantages and disadvantages of different types of management structure?

Type of Structure/Features	Advantages	Disadvantages
Tall Structure • there are usually many levels of management • managers will usually have narrow spans of control • management posts tend to be specialised	• it should be easier for managers to supervise staff • there are likely to be many opportunities for promotion • employees are more likely to know their immediate boss • employees are more likely to know the scope of their duties and responsibilities	• employees may feel undervalued and far removed from the real decision-making • employees may not get the opportunity to suggest ideas or show initiative • decision-making may be slow • it may take time to communicate decisions throughout the organisation • the management structure may be costly with many levels of highly-paid posts • may lead to complicated channels of communication with very formal procedures
Flat Structure • few levels of management • managers have wider spans of control	• employees are given more authority and responsibility – they are likely to feel more motivated • employees are more likely to be able to show initiative • employees are more likely to be involved in key decision-making • communication channels are likely to be less complicated and less formal – communication is likely to be more efficient • should take less time to reach decisions and for the organisation to react to situations • should take less time to communicate decisions throughout the organisation	• workloads of employees are likely to increase – possibility of stress • employees may need training to carry out new/wider responsibilities • where the span of control is too wide, employees may feel isolated or ignored • employees may not be able to meet with their line manager on a regular basis • likely to be fewer opportunities for promotion to management posts

What is a chain of command?

The way in which instructions are passed down through the various levels is known as the **chain of command**.

Each level through which instructions are passed can be seen as a link in the chain – having more levels of management leads to more links in the chain of command. Instructions should be passed down through each level within the organisation.

In the Admin Department the Admin Director gives instructions to the Admin Manager and the Admin Manager gives instructions to Sam. Sam gives instructions to the Assistants and the Receptionist. That is the chain of command.

> **Chain of Command** = the way in which instructions (commands) are passed down from one level of post to another within an organisation

What are the main types of relationship within an organisation?

There are two main types of relationship within an organisation:

Line Relationship
These exist between line managers and the staff immediately below them. Members of staff are accountable to their line manager for any actions or decisions they take. Line relationships are shown by the vertical lines on an organisation chart and stretch down through the whole organisation.

Lateral Relationship
These exist between employees who are on the same level and who report to the same line manager. The employees cannot give instructions to each other or to staff outwith their own spans of control.

The Sales and Marketing Director has a line relationship with the Sales Manager and the Marketing Manager. The Sales Manager and the Marketing Manager have a lateral relationship with each other.

How may organisations change?

Organisations are unlikely to remain the same year after year. The internal structure of an organisation may require to be changed (restructured) because the organisation is expanding or contracting.

Cause of Restructuring	Features	Effect on Organisation Chart
growth *Perth Daily Echo* Made4IT wins £2m order from Germany – 50 new jobs	• the organisation increases the amount and/or range of products/services sold • more staff are employed to meet increased sales • the organisation may have to increase the size of its premises	• more staff employed at the various levels • may result in new departments • may result in new specialist posts • may lead to more levels of management
downsizing *Perth Daily Echo* Jobs to go at Made4IT HQ	• the organisation reduces the number of staff employed without aiming to reduce output – some members of staff are likely to be made redundant • reduces the organisation's staffing costs	• main departments are likely to remain although departments may have to take on more duties • some posts are likely to disappear leading to fewer posts at each level • some workers will have increased responsibilities
delayering *Perth Daily Echo* Junior managers to be scrapped at Made4IT	• the organisation removes certain levels or layers of management posts • results in wider spans of control • should lead to management cost savings	• will result in a flatter structure • fewer levels of management posts • some workers will have increased responsibilities
outsourcing *Perth Daily Echo* Buying-in of security services likely to lead to job losses at Made4IT	• the organisation buys in services, eg computer software design, security or office cleaning, from another firm on a contract basis instead of getting its own staff to carry out the work • the organisation benefits from subcontracting specialists • the organisation can focus on its core (main) activities • may result from downsizing	• should result in a simpler organisation chart with fewer departments and/or fewer specialist members of staff

1b Introduction to Business Organisations: Key Functions of Departments within an Organisation

How are businesses organised?

Made4IT is a public limited company:
- the company's legal name ends with the abbreviation 'plc'
- the company is owned by its shareholders
- the shareholders have limited liability (the shareholders can lose no more than the cost of their shares)
- the shareholders are free to sell their shares or buy more
- the shareholders elect a group of Directors (the Board) at an Annual General Meeting to oversee the running of the company
- the price of the shares is quoted on the Stock Exchange.

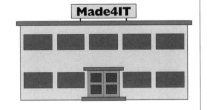

The structure of a public limited company (plc) is usually as follows:

```
                        Shareholders
                             |
                      Board of Directors
                             |
                       Chief Executive
        ┌──────────┬──────────┼──────────┬──────────┐
   Department 1  Department 2  Department 3  Department 4  Department 5
```

What is a functional area?

Organisations are usually structured around main activities. The activities are usually grouped into **functional areas** (or departments/divisions). In a large manufacturing organisation there are likely to be departments which carry out the functions of Purchases, Human Resources/Personnel, Finance, Production, Sales and Marketing, and Administration. There will usually be a Senior Manager (or Director) in charge of each area with the Senior Manager being responsible for the direction of her/his functional area within the organisation.

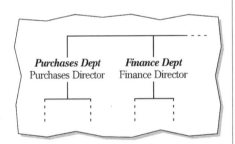

Functional Area = a key area of activity within an organisation, eg Human Resources/Personnel, Finance, Purchases, or Sales and Marketing

Department	Job Titles	Departmental Tasks/Activities
Purchases 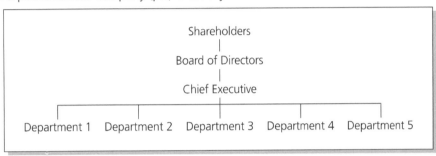	• Purchasing Director • Purchasing Manager • Chief Buyer • Quality Manager • Warehouse Supervisor • Stock Controller • Quality Controller • Buyer	• collects and processes purchase requisitions from departments • obtains quotations, catalogues and price lists from possible suppliers • agrees purchase prices and conditions (credit terms, delivery dates, warranties, etc) with suppliers • prepares purchase orders • receives and checks deliveries against delivery notes • keeps stock records • checks invoices against orders and goods received; authorises payment for goods

Department	Job Titles	Departmental Tasks/Activities
Human Resources/ Personnel	• Human Resources Director • Human Resources Manager • Recruitment Manager • Training Manager • Health and Safety Manager • Employee Relations Manager • Training Officer • Health and Safety Officer • Trainer • Health and Safety Assistant	• advertises vacancies • prepares job descriptions/person specifications • issues and collects job application forms • collects references • arranges and carries out interviews • prepares contracts of employment • keeps employee records (may be kept on a computerised database) • assists with staff appraisal • undertakes job grading • keeps accident records and reports • issues written/verbal warnings to employees • issues letters of dismissal • deals with staff welfare matters • organises training courses • meets with trade union representatives • advises on employment legislation

Job description = basic information about the job, ie job title, salary, to whom the employee is accountable and description of duties and responsibilities

Person specification = information on the type of person required, eg qualifications, experience, skills and qualities, and any special requirements, eg must have a driving licence

Department	Job Titles	Departmental Tasks/Activities
Finance	• Finance Director • Finance Manager • Chief Accountant • Financial Accountant • Management Accountant • Credit Controller • Invoice Supervisor • Invoice Clerk • Wages Assistant/Payroll Clerk • Accounts Assistant • Accounts Clerk	• checks invoices, credit notes and statements received from suppliers of goods and services • prepares invoices, credit notes and statements to be sent to customers • prepares cheques to be sent to suppliers • banks cash and cheques received from customers • prepares budgets (estimates of future income and expenditure or levels of sales/production) • prepares final accounts – Trading, Profit and Loss Account, Balance Sheet, etc • analyses financial information for management and shareholders • calculates wages and prepares payslips • completes tax returns

Invoice = the bill for goods bought on credit (informs the buyer of the amount owing, trade discount, VAT and any cash discount for prompt payment)

Credit Note = provides information on goods which have been returned by the buyer (gives cost of returned goods and states why the goods have been returned)

Statement = informs the buyer of the total amount owing at the end of a month (shows amount owing at the beginning of the month, plus invoices, less any credit notes and payments made, and the final balance)

Department	Job Titles	Departmental Tasks/Activities
Sales and Marketing	• Sales Director • Sales Manager • Marketing Manager • Area Sales Manager • Market Research Manager • Market Research Analyst • Advertising/Promotions Manager • Marketing Assistant • Sales Executive • Sales Representative • Salesperson • Telesales Assistant	• identifies potential new customers and products • visits customers • deals with enquiries for goods/services • sends out information, eg quotations, price lists and catalogues, to customers and potential customers • collects and processes orders from customers • keeps information on customers (may be kept on a computerised database) • deals with customer complaints • prepares and conducts consumer surveys • analyses completed market research questionnaires • prepares publicity, organises exhibitions, etc
Computing Services	• Computing Services Director • Computing Services Manager • Data Processing Manager • Data Analyst • Programmer • IT Support Technician • Computer Technician • Help Desk Operator	• advises on the purchase of ICT hardware (computers, scanners, printers, etc) and software (word processing, spreadsheet, database, desktop publishing [DTP], etc) • advises on the installation of networks (LANs, WANs, intranet and the Internet) • advises on ICT health and safety, and security issues • installs computer hardware, software and networks • rectifies hardware/software/network faults • maintains inventories of hardware/software • trials new hardware and software • trains/instructs employees in the use of ICT hardware/ software • constructs databases • puts security marks on to hardware • maintains user IDs and passwords
Administration	• Administration Director • Administration Manager • Office Manager • Administration Supervisor • Secretary • Computer Operator • Administrative Assistant • Word Processing Assistant • Mailroom Assistant • Reprographics Assistant • Receptionist • Stationery Stock Clerk • Audio Typist • Filing Clerk • Switchboard Operator • Office Junior	Deals with the following on a departmental or centralised basis: • word processing (preparation of letters, memos, reports, agendas, minutes, itineraries, etc) • desktop publishing (the preparation of leaflets, booklets, flyers, advertisements, etc) • incoming, outgoing and internal mail • secretarial services (dealing with phone calls, dealing with routine mail, managing diaries, taking minutes, making travel arrangements, filing correspondence, etc) • reception and switchboard • reprographics • manual and computerised databases • office supplies (supplying stationery to departments) • e-mail and faxes • petty cash and other financial records (possibly kept on spreadsheets)

2a The Working Environment: Office Layout

What are the main types of office layout?

Cellular (also known as Individual)

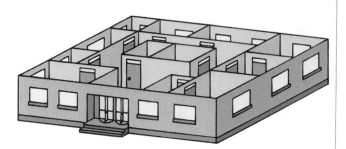

Cellular (or **Individual)** = consists of rooms in which an employee works on her/his own or with a few other employees

Advantages	Disadvantages
• as rooms are usually lockable it should be easier to restrict access to equipment or confidential information	• it is more difficult for a manager to supervise employees who are in a number of separate rooms
• employees are less likely to be distracted or have their work interrupted by other employees	• communication may be less efficient – it may be more difficult to organise meetings of employees from different departments
• offices can be used to hold confidential meetings or meetings with important customers/clients	• time may be wasted in passing information and work from one room to another
• encourages a team approach amongst those employees who share a room	• employees may feel isolated – they may not know where their work fits into the work of the organisation; they may not get to know other employees
• each room can be designed and equipped to suit the employees working in the room or the type of work being undertaken – employees can adjust heating, lighting, ventilation, etc	• individual rooms cost more to equip and redecorate; walls, doors and windows take up valuable (and expensive) space
• noisy office equipment can be placed in a separate room	• it may not be easy to increase or decrease size of work areas to match changes in the volume of work
• infections and illnesses are less easily spread through the organisation	• it is more difficult to create a relaxed and friendly atmosphere as line managers are likely to be in separate rooms
• it is easier for employees to personalise their work area with plants, photographs, etc	• it is more difficult to introduce and maintain standard procedures

The illustration on page 15 shows the ground floor of Made4IT's offices in the early 1990s.

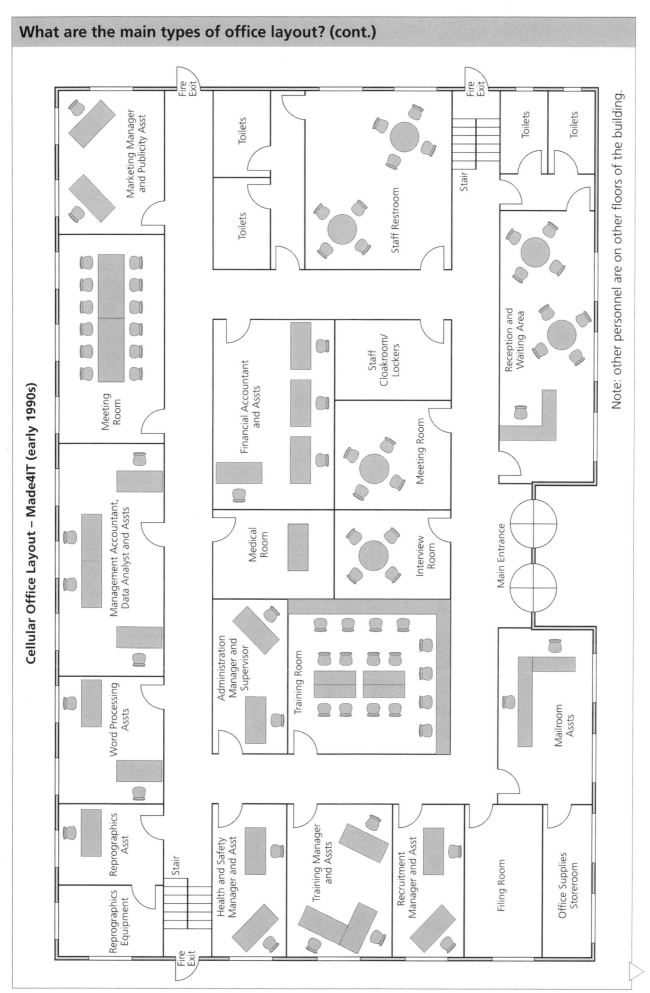

Cellular Office Layout – Made4IT (early 1990s)

Marketing Manager and Publicity Asst

Meeting Room

Management Accountant, Data Analyst and Assts

Word Processing Assts

Reprographics Asst

Reprographics Equipment

Stair

Fire Exit

Toilets

Toilets

Staff Restroom

Financial Accountant and Assts

Staff Cloakroom/Lockers

Meeting Room

Medical Room

Interview Room

Administration Manager and Supervisor

Training Room

Health and Safety Manager and Asst

Training Manager and Assts

Recruitment Manager and Asst

Filing Room

Office Supplies Storeroom

Fire Exit

Stair

Fire Exit

Toilets

Toilets

Reception and Waiting Area

Main Entrance

Mailroom Assts

Note: other personnel are on other floors of the building.

Open Plan (one type of Open Plan is known as 'Landscaped')

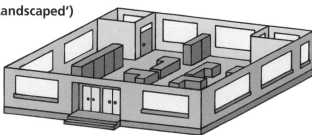

> **Open Plan** = consists of a large area where many employees work together
>
> **Landscaped** = a very large open plan area where all the office activities are undertaken

Employees may work on their own or be grouped to carry out common activities. Dividers, soundproof screens, furniture, filing cabinets and plants may be used to give some privacy. Interlocking desks may be joined together in a number of different patterns to form group workstations.

The décor and furnishings are usually bright, modern and of high quality. Thought will have been given as to how information is passed from one section to another within the organisation. Activities will be grouped to ensure that time wasted in passing information is kept to a minimum.

Advantages	Disadvantages
• line managers should find it easier to supervise employees	• employees may find it difficult to concentrate on their work because of background noise
• it should be easier to organise meetings of groups of employees	• employees may be distracted or have their work interrupted by other employees or by through-traffic
• less time should be wasted in passing information and work from one group of employees to another	• it may be more difficult to restrict access by unauthorised staff to equipment or confidential information
• employees are likely to have a better understanding of how their area of work fits into the overall work of the organisation	• there are likely to be fewer suitable areas for holding confidential or important meetings
• less space is wasted with fewer walls and doors; lighting, heating and cleaning should be less expensive and easier to organise	• infections and illnesses can be more easily spread amongst employees
• the size of work areas can be increased or decreased to match changes in the volume of work	• likely to be less wall space for departmental information (charts, tables, pictures, etc)
• a more relaxed and friendly atmosphere can be created with employees and line managers working in the same area – should lead to increased cooperation across sections of the organisation	• private offices may still be required for senior staff
• equipment, eg photocopiers, fax machines and scanners, can be more easily shared	• standard lighting, heating and ventilation may not suit all activities or all employees

The illustration on page 17 shows the ground floor of Made4IT's offices in the late 1990s after it moved to an Open Plan layout in a different building.

Open Plan Office Layout – Made4IT (late 1990s)

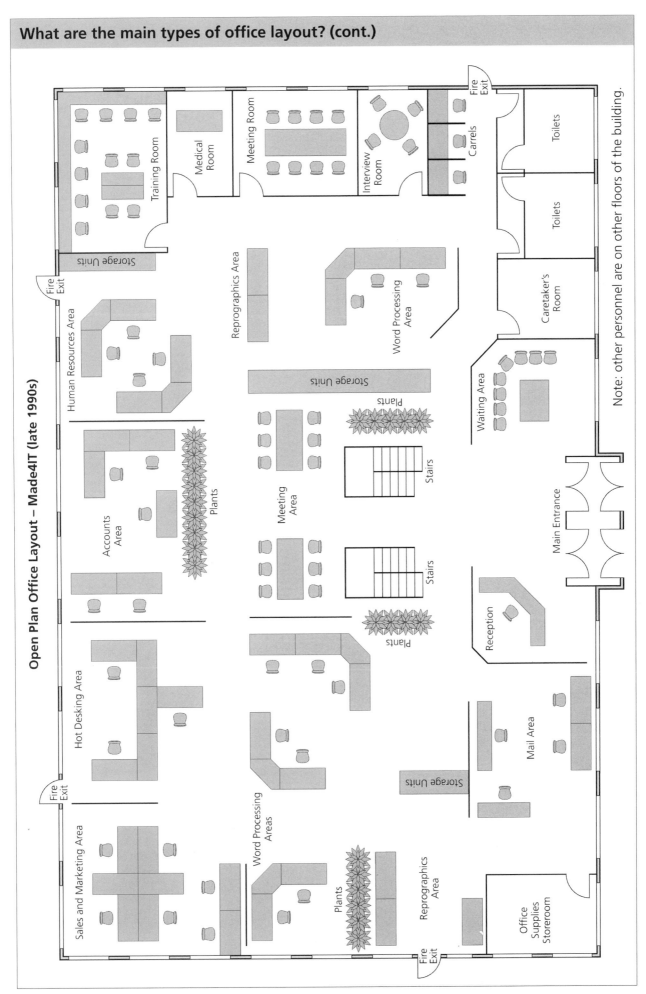

Note: other personnel are on other floors of the building.

What factors should be considered when deciding on the layout of an office?

The layout chosen by an organisation will depend upon:
- the size of the organisation – the number of employees
- whether the organisation is expanding or contracting
- the type of work undertaken by the organisation
- the accommodation available to the organisation
- the financial resources available to the organisation.

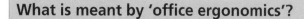

The layout chosen should:
- be adaptable to meet changes in the type or volume of work
- provide sufficient work and storage space
- take account of the flow of work – time taken to pass information from one section to another should be kept to a minimum
- allow employees to move about easily – passageways should be wide and free from obstruction
- be economical to maintain, ie to decorate, keep clean and heat
- provide easy access to services, eg power points and phone sockets
- provide easy access to equipment, eg filing cabinets, photocopiers, printers and fax machines
- provide security for equipment and information.

What is meant by 'office ergonomics'?

Ergonomics looks at how the working environment (including furniture, equipment, décor, heating, lighting, ventilation, noise, work activities and procedures) affects the work of employees.

Improving the working environment should:
- improve employee morale and commitment to the organisation
- increase output and improve efficiency
- reduce accidents and injuries
- reduce sickness and absenteeism
- reduce stress.

What features of office furniture are important?

As well as giving careful consideration to the layout of the office, organisations need to think about:
- the type of furniture to be used
- the layout of furniture and equipment
- the layout of workstations.

Office Furniture
- **Desks**
  - size and shape of work surface should suit the work to be undertaken
  - mobile pedestal units (with drawers or shelves) may be placed beneath work surfaces
  - consideration should be given to height, depth, width, weight, mobility, etc
  - work surface should be non-reflective
  - should match and be able to be combined with other office furniture

- **Workstations**
  - L-shaped desk: an employee can carry out computer work on one part of the desk and turn to the other part to do paperwork, make phone calls, etc
  - consideration should be given to cable management – some workstations have channels to store/hide cables
  - desks of different sizes and shapes may be bought to allow for a variety of layouts

What features of office furniture are important? (cont.)

• **Storage units**
Metal storage units provide some protection against fire and flood.

 bookcase
(used for holding reference books, publications, reports, manuals, etc)

 vertical filing cabinet
(used for holding correspondence and other business documents)

 lateral filing cabinet
(used for holding a wide range of business documents)

 multi-drawer cabinet
(used for storing loose papers/forms, thick files, odd-sized documents, manuals, etc)

 storage cabinet/ cupboard
(used for storing stationery supplies, box files, folders, etc)

 mobile pedestal
(used for storing stationery and small items of office equipment [stapler, paper punch, scissors, etc] required at a workstation)

 card index box
(used for holding index cards on customers, suppliers, employees, etc)

 cardboard box file
(used for storing papers which have not been fully dealt with)

 metal box file
(used as a mini-filing cabinet and when transporting files)

• **Chairs**
Minimum standards are laid down in the Health and Safety (Display Screen Equipment) Regulations 1992.

Ⓐ seat back adjustable for height and tilt (should provide support to lower back)

Ⓑ swivel action allows operator to turn easily

Ⓒ adjustable for height (new models have a gas lift mechanism which allows the height of the chair to be adjusted at the touch of a lever)

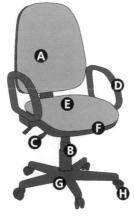

Ⓓ arm rests (except for keyboard operators)

Ⓔ cushioned for comfort

Ⓕ seat sloping to front to reduce pressure on thighs

Ⓖ 5-star base provides stability

Ⓗ castors allow easy movement of chair

How should office furniture and equipment be set out?

The layout of furniture and equipment should:
- be suited to the type of work to be undertaken
- make the best use of the space available
- be flexible to allow for changing needs
- provide an attractive and pleasant working environment
- provide safe working conditions – furniture and equipment must satisfy health and safety requirements
- allow employees to move easily between work areas
- keep noise levels to a minimum
- provide for easy access to phone sockets and power sources
- make good use of heating, lighting and ventilation
- provide for restricted access to certain areas, eg where confidential work needs to be undertaken or important meetings need to be held.

Activity	Requirements
Administrative and Clerical Work 	- large work surface suitable for doing written work, handling papers and using a computer - access to power points, phone sockets and computer network - soundproof screens to reduce noise and to provide privacy for on-screen confidential work - access to storage units
Meetings and Interviews 	- privacy – either a separate room or an area sectioned off with soundproof screens - large table(s) for meetings; coffee table for interviews - comfortable seating - access to audio/visual equipment - pleasant surroundings (pictures, plants, etc) - tea- and coffee-making facilities

How should a workstation be organised?

Workstations should:
- have a cable management system (channels on desk, wall or floor to house unsightly, and potentially dangerous, cables)
- be free from clutter (especially if other employees have to use the workstation) – use should be made of drawers, filing trays, desk tidies, book holders, etc
- have all working materials (paperclips, stapler, 'post-its', envelopes, etc) close to hand
- have easy access to a phone, especially where the employee may have to answer her/his line manager's incoming phone calls
- have drawers available for the storage of materials.

What are the implications of developments in ICT on work practices and the layout of workstations?

Traditionally employees have worked at their employer's premises. Advances in ICT are, however, allowing more and more employees to work whilst:
- at home
- travelling, eg on trains and planes
- on customers' premises
- in hotel rooms.

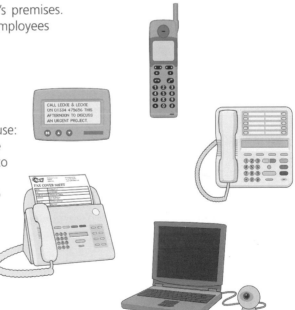

When away from the employer's premises, employees can use:
- laptop (portable) computers with applications software (eg word processing, spreadsheet, database and DTP) to process information
- computers to receive and send e-mail messages and to access information on websites
- mobile phones to receive and send messages
- voicemail and telephone answering machines to receive and record messages
- fax machines to receive and send information
- pagers to receive messages or to be alerted to phone their employer
- videoconferencing facilities to hold meetings.

What is homeworking/teleworking?

Homeworking is where employees, as part of their conditions of employment, work at home some or all of the time. The proportion of time spent working at home will depend on the type of work the employee does.

Homeworking is not suitable for jobs where regular face-to-face discussions and meetings with other employees are required. It can be suitable for jobs where an employee spends a great deal of time on her/his own working on a computer (eg writers, journalists, researchers, designers, computer consultants and accountants). Administrative tasks which involve the keying in of vast amounts of information may also be suitable for homeworking.

Work which is undertaken at home and transmitted to the employer using ICT equipment and phone links is known as teleworking.

Advantages and Disadvantages of Homeworking/Teleworking

Advantages	Disadvantages
• less space required at the employer's premises – likely to lead to significant cost savings especially at high-priced city centre sites	• loss of close control over employees who are working at home – employees need to be able to work on their own without supervision
• employees waste less time in travelling to work – should lead to increased output	• cost of purchasing, using and maintaining ICT equipment
• increases in transport costs and parking charges will have little effect on employees	• more difficult to ensure that ICT equipment and home workstations satisfy health and safety requirements
• employer may be able to keep employing staff who might otherwise leave, eg following birth of child	• more difficult to organise training in the use of equipment and software, and in aspects of safety
• organisation can employ workers who might not be able to work in the office, eg workers with certain types of physical disability	• more difficult to provide advice and support in the use of ICT equipment
• employee motivation may be increased with employees given more responsibility for managing their own time	• employees may not be available for meetings at short notice
• should be less stressful for employees	• employees will miss out on social aspects of work – employees may feel remote from the employer
• employer and employee have greater flexibility in arranging working hours	

What is hot desking?

Where a significant amount of work is undertaken on a homeworking/teleworking basis there is no need to provide all employees with a desk or workstation at the organisation's premises. Instead, organisations may provide a number of '**hot desks**' for those employees who occasionally require to come into the office to do some work. This saves valuable space and money, and should maximise the use of expensive ICT equipment. Over time the organisation should be able to work out the ideal number of hot desks to be provided.

What is hot desking? (cont.)

Hot desks are desks (or workstations) which may be booked in advance (usually on a half-day basis) for use by any employee. An employee who wishes to use a hot desk, but has not booked one in advance, will have to report to a reception area to check whether one is available. Employees may also book '**hot rooms**' to hold meetings with customers/clients or other employees. Some organisations provide meeting areas with tea- and coffee-making facilities where employees can meet to have a chat on a less formal basis.

Hot desks have a standard layout and equipment – usually a large work area with a computer (with standard applications and access to the organisation's computer network), operator chair and phone. It is, of course, important that an employee clears away any materials she/he has been using so that the hot desk is ready for the next employee to use.

Some organisations may provide small booths (**carrels**) for employees to work in. Carrels provide more privacy, and fewer distractions, for employees.

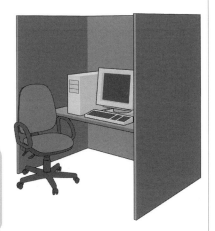

Organisations may also provide '**touchdown areas**' for employees who require to make a brief visit to the office, eg to send an e-mail or fax. Touchdown areas may take the form of a coffee bar with high tables and stools. Unlike hot desks, touchdown areas are not bookable. Such areas are meant to be used for very short periods of time on a drop-in basis.

> **Hot desk** = a desk or workstation, equipped with standard equipment, which may be used by employees who need to visit the organisation to undertake some work
>
> **Carrel** = a small booth where an employee works on her/his own

How can work be organised?

Alternatives to full-time, 9 am to 5 pm, permanent contracts include:

Organisation of Employment	Features
Job-sharing **Word Processing Assistant** Job-share partner required to work Tuesdays and Wednesdays. Apply Made4IT	• employees share a full-time job between them • each employee is paid a proportion of the full-time salary • suitable for employees who do not wish to take on a full-time work commitment • if one of the job-share partners is off sick or on holiday then the other job-share partner might be available to take her/his place • not suitable for all types of employment, eg senior management posts
Flexitime ARRIVE 09:30	• employees are given some flexibility in organising their starting and finishing times – allows employees to start/leave early or late or take a longer lunch-break • employees are required to be at work each day during **core time**, eg 10.00 am – 12.00 noon and 2.00 pm – 4.00 pm • should improve timekeeping • allows employees to avoid heavy road traffic and arrange service appointments (electricity, gas, car repairs, etc) • employees have to 'clock in' and 'clock out' by inserting cards in electronic recording equipment to record times of arrival and departure • should lead to a reduction in overtime payments • if employees build up sufficient credit hours they may take a half-day or a day off in lieu

What are the implications for management of changes in office layout or work practices?

The following may have to be considered by management if changes are proposed to office layout or work practices:

- need to alter the premises because of changes in the provision of workstations, heating, lighting, cabling, power supply, phone outlets, etc
- purchase of additional accommodation, furniture and equipment
- provision of hot desks, hot rooms or touchdown areas
- maintenance of ICT equipment used by homeworkers/teleworkers
- introduction of new/revised work procedures
- provision of staff training
- safety and security of equipment and information
- health, safety and welfare of members of staff
- management of change (see below).

Any changes should be implemented carefully and sensitively by:
- planning how the changes will be introduced
- introducing change gradually
- informing employees fully about what is happening
- involving employees at each stage
- explaining to employees how the changes are likely to affect their work and what the benefits will be
- consulting and negotiating with employee representatives (eg trade unions)
- reassuring employees of their value to the organisation
- monitoring the process of change at each stage
- providing appropriate training.

2b The Working Environment: Safe Working Practices and Procedures

What are some of the potential hazards to be found in offices?

Potential hazards in offices are numerous. Major injuries may be caused by:
- slips or trips (eg slipping on slippery surface or falling over an obstruction)
- falling from a height (eg falling down stairs or falling from a chair)
- being struck by a moving or flying object (eg being struck by a door or being struck by an object falling from a shelf or table)
- poor handling, lifting or carrying of an object.

Potential hazard = something about the working environment, equipment or working practices which may cause harm

To work safely, employees should:
- position filing cabinets away from doors and passageways
- fill vertical filing cabinets from the bottom up – this will make them more stable
- not store heavy materials and boxes on top of filing cabinets – stack frequently-used materials on shelves within easy reach
- not stand on chairs to reach boxes – use a stepladder or mobile step (kick stool)

- keep liquids away from computer equipment – liquids may cause damage to equipment or start electrical fires
- position desks to avoid trailing cables or use cable covers or a cable management system attached to desk or wall
- not overload electricity sockets
- report faulty lights
- request desk lighting if necessary

- keep all chair legs on the floor
- empty wastepaper bins regularly – store waste materials in fireproof place until collected
- use a damp sponge or roller to seal envelopes to prevent cutting tongue
- smoke only in designated areas (if they must smoke) and use appropriate bins for disposing of matches, ash and cigarette ends
- never prop open fire doors

What are some of the potential hazards to be found in offices? (cont.)

To work safely, employees should also:
- pick up dropped objects from the floor – people can easily trip over them
- immediately mop up spilt liquids – use 'Wet Floor' signs
- be trained in how to lift and carry materials – never try to carry too much
- keep passageways free from obstacles

- position computer screens so as to avoid glare from sunshine or lighting
- attach anti-glare filter screen to VDU (visual display unit) and/or close blinds to reduce glare
- ensure windows are fitted with security catches
- ensure alternative ventilation systems are provided or consider repositioning workstations

- not attempt to sort equipment unless fully trained to do so
- never open electrical equipment whilst the equipment is still plugged in
- not let ties or jewellery fall into equipment
- report loose flooring – it should be temporarily taped down and repaired as soon as possible

What should an employee do if the office equipment being used develops a fault?

Before using equipment, the employee should have received appropriate training and have been authorised to use the equipment.

If a fault develops the employee should:
- switch off electrically-operated equipment and pull out the plug from the mains socket – the employee must not attempt to use the equipment until it has been repaired
- put a notice on the equipment to inform other staff that it is faulty and that the fault has been reported
- report the fault to the appropriate person (line manager, maintenance personnel, etc) – a Hazard/Fault Report Form (see page 27) should be completed
- not attempt to fix the equipment – fingers must never be placed inside the equipment or a screwdriver or other object poked into the equipment.

What should an employee do if the office equipment being used develops a fault? (cont.)

MADE 4 IT

HAZARD/FAULT REPORT FORM

Please complete this form for any identified hazard/fault and pass it to your supervisor.

ROOM NO.	A8
DESCRIPTION OF HAZARD/FAULT	When using the computer the monitor began to make a crackling noise. After a few seconds the monitor went blank and smoke began to pour out the back of the monitor.
IDENTIFY MACHINE/EQUIPMENT HAZARD/FAULT RELATES TO	Monitor of computer No. AM/14 in the Word Processing Section
REPORTED BY	Pauline Stuart, Word Processing Assistant
DATE	Monday, 22 May 2000
IF REMEDIAL/CORRECTIVE ACTION TAKEN, PLEASE DESCRIBE	I immediately switched off the computer at the mains socket and removed the plug. I placed a notice on the monitor stating that it was faulty and should not be used until repaired.
SIGNATURE OF SUPERVISOR	Sam Ryan

What first-aid procedures should be in place?

If an employee witnesses an accident at work she/he should:
- contact one of the organisation's 'first-aiders' or the emergency services (a first-aider is someone who has undertaken an approved first-aid training course and has been awarded a first-aid certificate recognised by the Health and Safety Executive [HSE] – first-aiders are required to take refresher courses every three years)
- reassure the injured person that appropriate action is being taken
- talk to the injured person – try to keep the injured person calm
- wait with the injured person until the first-aider arrives
- complete an Accident Report Form and enter information in an Accident Book (see examples on page 28).

Employees who have not received first-aid training should not attempt to treat injured persons – they could make the situation worse!

ACCIDENT REPORT FORM

Report of an accident or injury to a person on the organisation's premises. This form must be completed in all cases of accident or injury and submitted to your line manager.

Name of injured person	*Jenny Kerr*
Date of birth	*22/08/81*
Position in the organisation	*Receptionist*
Date and time of accident	*Wednesday, 17 May 2000 at 1245 hours*
Brief description of accident (continue on separate sheet if required)	*Jenny tripped over a briefcase and fell to the floor.*
Brief description of activity at time of accident	*When showing a visitor to a meeting room, Jenny tripped over the visitor's briefcase which had been left on the floor.*
Place of accident	*Reception*
Details of injury	*Hurt her right knee – difficulty in walking.*
First-aid treatment (if given)	*Knee strapped.*
Was the injured person taken to hospital/doctor?	*Yes – taken to hospital*
Name(s) and position(s) of person(s) present when accident occurred	*Sam Ryan, Admin Supervisor and appointed first-aider.*

Signature of person reporting accident: *Sam Ryan*   Date: *18 May 2000*

ACCIDENT BOOK

DATE	TIME	LOCATION	NAME OF INJURED PERSON	WITNESS	DETAILS OF ACCIDENT AND ACTION TAKEN
12/01/2000	1315	Marketing	Gerry McQuade	James Dignan	Fell off ladder and received gash to head. Head bandaged. Taken to hospital.
09/02/2000	0940	Marketing	Ruth Chalmers	Margaret Joyce	Fainted whilst at workstation. Kept warm whilst recovering. Taken to doctor.
17/03/2000	1120	Finance	Paul Johnson	Duncan Simpson	Hurt back when moving desk. Taken home. Is to see own doctor.
17/05/2000	1245	Reception	Jenny Kerr	Sam Ryan	Tripped over briefcase and hurt right knee. Knee strapped. Taken to hospital.

What should be kept in a first-aid box?

There is no standard list of contents. The following is the minimum stock of first-aid items suggested by the Health and Safety Executive:
- a leaflet giving general guidance on first-aid, eg HSE leaflet *Basic Advice on First-aid at Work*
- 20 individually wrapped sterile adhesive dressings (assorted sizes)
- 2 sterile eye pads
- 4 individually wrapped triangular bandages
- 6 safety pins
- 6 medium-sized individually wrapped sterile unmedicated wound dressings
- 2 large individually wrapped sterile unmedicated wound dressings
- 1 pair of disposable gloves.

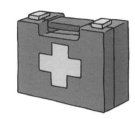

Tablets and medicines should **not** be kept in a first-aid box.

What are the main health issues when using display screen equipment?

Health Problem	Action to be Taken

eye fatigue and **headaches**	• check and adjust as necessary:
	  • clarity of items on screen (adjust brightness/contrast controls, clean screen as necessary)
	  • glare on screen (use of blinds and anti-glare filter screen)
	  • screen flicker
	  • position of VDU and copyholder
	• check whether operator has had a recent eye test (provide with spectacles as necessary)
	• check noise and lighting levels (provide additional lighting at workstation as necessary)
	• check that the operator is taking regular short breaks from the workstation
	• check that the operator has received appropriate health and safety training in using the equipment
	• check heat and humidity (make sure that the work area is well ventilated)

body aches and pains including repetitive strain injury (RSI)	In addition to above, check and adjust as necessary: • layout of the workstation • position of chair, work surface and footrest • availability and suitability of wristrests.
stress	In addition to above: • check that the operator has been properly trained in the use of the hardware and software • check the operator's workload – get others to share workload as necessary • try to vary the operator's work.

Below is an example of an ideal ICT workstation.

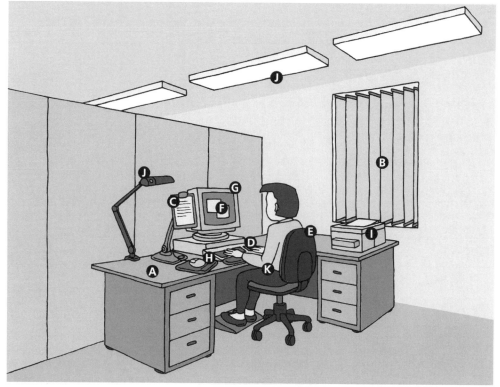

A work surface
- allows flexible arrangement of equipment
- large
- glare-free
- sufficient leg room below work surface to allow for change in posture

B windows
- fitted with suitable screening to allow adjustment to level of daylight on workstation

C document holder
- documents at same level and distance as the screen
- stable and adjustable

D keyboard
- detachable – operator can position the keyboard to suit her/himself
- tiltable
- matt surface to avoid glare
- key tops legible
- wristrest

E chair
- adjustable for height
- seat back adjustable for height and tilt
- stable base

F software
- suitable for task
- user-friendly
- appropriate to experience of user

G VDU
- well-defined characters
- adequate size
- stable image (no flickering)
- adjustable (for brightness and/or contrast, swivel and tilt)
- glare-free

H mouse
- on same level as keyboard
- mouse mat with wristrest

I printer
- distracting noise to be minimised

J lighting
- must be adequate
- no direct/indirect glare or reflections
- no flickering lights
- additional lighting at workstation

K positioning of operator
- upper and lower arms at approximately right angles
- eye level in line with top of VDU
- face directly in front of the screen
- knees level with hips
- lower back supported
- upper arms relaxed at sides
- wrists straight (in line with hand and forearm)
- feet flat on the floor or on a footrest

How does an employee maintain a safe working environment?

- follow organisation's health and safety guidelines
- follow safe practices when using office equipment
- check the position and layout of the workstation – identify potential hazards and make appropriate suggestions to line manager
- keep work area tidy – use desk tidies, book holders, trays, etc
- file documents regularly – use in/out-trays, filing cabinets and other storage units
- don't stack papers on equipment or place materials where they could fall or be knocked off desks
- use wastepaper bins provided – do not overfill bins
- handle and store dangerous materials with care (cleaning fluids, toner, etc)
- don't block cooling vents on computers and other office equipment
- don't drink at workstation
- wear finger guards when handling stacks of paper; use a damp sponge or roller to seal envelopes; don't mix drawing pins with paperclips, etc

What emergency and evacuation procedures should be in place?

The following is the fire/evacuation procedure for Made4IT – procedures in other organisations may differ slightly.

FIRE/EVACUATION PROCEDURE

Instructions to Staff and Visitors
Action to be taken in case of fire or other emergency.
Assembly Point: Rear Car Park – Area 4

If you discover a fire:

1 Warn others in the immediate area of the fire.

Go to the nearest fire alarm point and sound the fire alarm (the caretaker will phone the Fire Brigade).

2 Only attempt to contain the fire (using the fire extinguishers available) if you have been fully trained in fire fighting.

Shut the doors and, if possible, the windows of the room where the fire is located.

On hearing the fire alarm sound:

3 Leave the building immediately by the nearest exit.

4 Obey the instructions of the person appointed to evacuate the floor of the building.
DO NOT USE THE LIFT.
DO NOT STOP TO PUT ON COATS OR COLLECT PERSONAL BELONGINGS.
WALK BRISKLY – DO NOT RUN OR PANIC.
IF YOU HAVE A VISITOR ESCORT HER/HIM TO THE ASSEMBLY POINT.
DO NOT RE-ENTER THE BUILDING TO LOOK FOR SOMEONE OR FOR ANY OTHER REASON UNTIL THE SAFETY OFFICER GIVES YOU PERMISSION TO DO SO.

5 Report to the appropriate person at the assembly point where a roll call will be taken.

THIS NOTICE MUST BE DISPLAYED IN ALL ROOMS/WORK AREAS, ON NOTICE BOARDS AND BESIDE FIRE ALARM POINTS.

STAFF MUST FAMILIARISE THEMSELVES WITH THE ABOVE PROCEDURE.

What health and safety legislation is likely to affect office employees?

The law protects the health and safety of people (employees and the self-employed) at work and people in the workplace (whether employees or visitors to the workplace). The law is enforced through a series of Acts.

> **Workplace** = the place where work is undertaken, eg a factory, shop, office, hospital or worksite

The main Acts are:
- the Health and Safety at Work Act (HASAWA) 1974
- the Health and Safety (First-Aid) Regulations 1981
- the Health and Safety (Display Screen Equipment) Regulations 1992
- the Reporting of Injuries, Diseases and Dangerous Occurrences Regulations (RIDDOR) 1995

Health and safety legislation is enforced by an 'enforcing authority', ie the Health and Safety Executive (HSE) or the Local Authority Environmental Health Department.

What are the main provisions of the Health and Safety at Work Act (HASAWA) 1974?

Under this Act both employers and employees have legal responsibilities.

Responsibilities of Employer	*Responsibilities of Employee*
To ensure the health, safety and welfare at work of their employees. This includes: • providing safe entrance and exit from work • ensuring safe methods of working • ensuring safe working conditions • ensuring that equipment is safe and properly maintained • arranging for the safe use, storage and movement of hazardous substances • providing protective clothing where necessary • providing information and training on health and safety • preparing and updating organisational health and safety policy – the policy should be circulated to all employees • allowing the appointment of safety representatives by a recognised trade union.	• to take reasonable care of own health and safety and of the health and safety of others who may be affected by the work of the employee • to cooperate with the employer on health and safety matters • not to misuse or interfere with anything provided for the employee's health and safety

What are the main provisions of the Health and Safety (First-Aid) Regulations 1981?

Employers must:
- ensure that an 'appointed' person is available to take charge of first-aid arrangements when someone is injured or falls ill and to look after first-aid equipment
- ensure that a first-aider is designated – a first-aider can also take on the duties of an appointed person
- ensure that a suitably stocked first-aid box is available
- ensure that a record is kept of all incidents
- inform employees about first-aid arrangements, ie names and locations of appointed persons and first-aiders, and location of first-aid box.

What are the main provisions of the Health and Safety (Display Screen Equipment) Regulations 1992?

Employers are required to:
- analyse workstations (includes equipment, furniture and work environment) and assess and reduce risks
- ensure that workstations meet minimum requirements
- provide users with training on how to use VDUs and workstations safely (including making adjustments to workstations so as to avoid health problems)
- organise the daily work of VDU users so that there are regular rest breaks or changes of activity
- arrange and pay for regular eyesight tests for VDU users – the employer is required to pay for any spectacles or lenses which are required as a result of VDU use at work.

What are the main provisions of the Reporting of Injuries, Diseases and Dangerous Occurrences Regulations (RIDDOR) 1995?

Death or Major Injury

If an incident causes death or major injury to an employee or member of the public, the employer must:
- notify the enforcing authority without delay (eg by phone)
- forward an accident report form to the enforcing authority within ten days.

Over three-day Injury

If an incident stops someone doing their normal job for more than three days, the employer must:
- forward an accident report form to the enforcing authority within ten days.

Disease

If a doctor informs an employer that an employee suffers from a reportable work-related disease, the employer must:
- forward a disease report form to the enforcing authority within ten days.

Dangerous Occurrence

If something happens which did not, but could have, resulted in a reportable injury, the employer must:
- notify the enforcing authority without delay
- forward an accident report form to the enforcing authority within ten days.

Keeping Records

Employers must keep records (copies of forms sent to the enforcing authority of any reportable injury, disease or dangerous occurrence) for three years after the date of the incident. These records must include:
- the date and method of reporting
- the date, time and place of the event
- the personal details of those involved
- a brief description of the nature of the event or disease.

2c The Working Environment: Reception Services

Why is the way in which visitors are dealt with important to the wellbeing of an organisation?

The receptionist is often the first person in an organisation that a potential customer comes across – first impressions count! What the receptionist says and does (or doesn't say and do) can influence the success of the organisation.

The way in which visitors are dealt with and the layout of the reception area give an impression of the overall efficiency of the organisation and the care the organisation shows to customers.

What are the qualities and duties of a receptionist?

Qualities	Duties
• thorough knowledge of the organisation – layout, main activities and key personnel • good communication skills (attentive, with a clear voice and good handwriting) • tidy and well groomed • friendly and helpful • polite • calm • patient • tactful • discreet	• welcomes visitors to the organisation • operates the switchboard (receives phone calls and, where appropriate, makes phone calls) • takes and passes on messages • contacts members of staff to inform them of a visitor's arrival • directs visitors to areas/rooms within building • ensures that visitors enter information in the Visitors' Book • signs for mail, packages and parcels • makes sure that the reception area is well organised (magazines kept tidy and up to date, dirty cups removed, flowers and plants watered, etc) • other duties may include: operating the telephone answering machine and fax machine, and word processing

How should visitors be received by the receptionist?

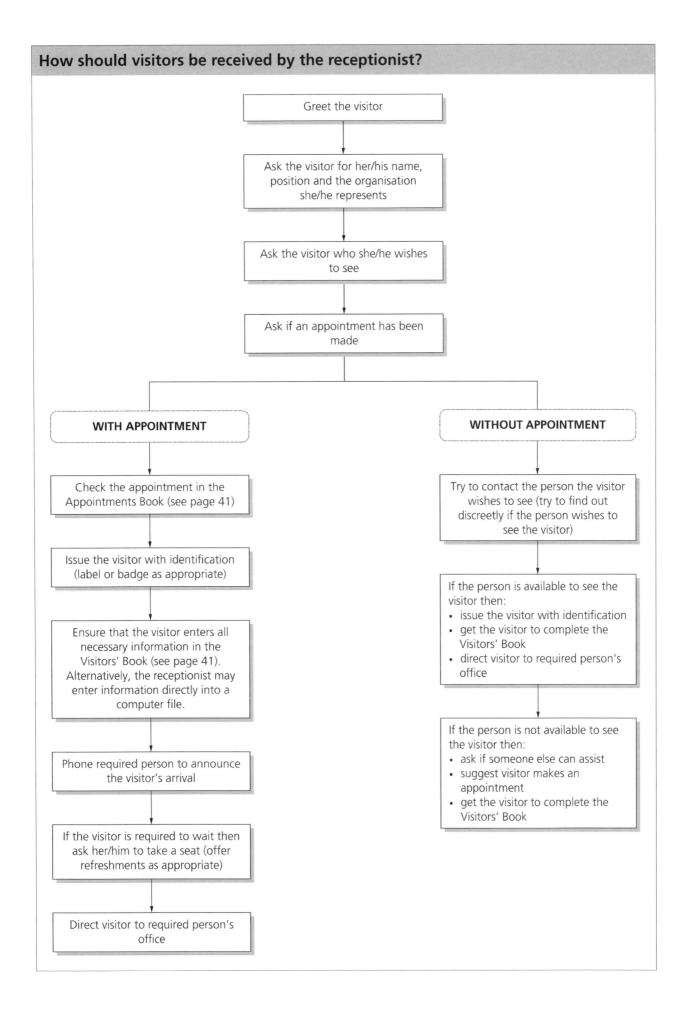

Greet the visitor

↓

Ask the visitor for her/his name, position and the organisation she/he represents

↓

Ask the visitor who she/he wishes to see

↓

Ask if an appointment has been made

WITH APPOINTMENT

Check the appointment in the Appointments Book (see page 41)

↓

Issue the visitor with identification (label or badge as appropriate)

↓

Ensure that the visitor enters all necessary information in the Visitors' Book (see page 41). Alternatively, the receptionist may enter information directly into a computer file.

↓

Phone required person to announce the visitor's arrival

↓

If the visitor is required to wait then ask her/him to take a seat (offer refreshments as appropriate)

↓

Direct visitor to required person's office

WITHOUT APPOINTMENT

Try to contact the person the visitor wishes to see (try to find out discreetly if the person wishes to see the visitor)

↓

If the person is available to see the visitor then:
- issue the visitor with identification
- get the visitor to complete the Visitors' Book
- direct visitor to required person's office

↓

If the person is not available to see the visitor then:
- ask if someone else can assist
- suggest visitor makes an appointment
- get the visitor to complete the Visitors' Book

How should the reception area be set out?

A reception area located near the main entrance

B large reception desk with visitors' records

C computer (access to electronic diaries), fax machine, telephone answering machine, phone switchboard and public address system

D waiting area

E toilet facilities

F access and facilities for disabled visitors

G well decorated and furnished (coffee table, comfortable chairs, good lighting, pictures, plants, etc)

H receptionist may wear a uniform

I reading material (publicity material about the organisation or general magazines and newspapers)

J drinks (tea, coffee and water) should be available

K organisation chart

L CCTV (closed circuit television)

M photographs of key personnel

N certificates and awards given to organisation

What is an electronic diary?

- a computer application which allows users to check, enter and store information on future appointments
- space may be provided for a 'to do' list and for notes to be entered beside each appointment, eg papers to be taken to a meeting
- the electronic diaries of several people can be searched to find a suitable date for all to meet
- the application will not allow two meetings to be scheduled for the same time on the same date
- regular meetings, eg a meeting on the first Monday of each month, need be keyed in only once – the application will then repeat the entry automatically
- names, addresses, phone numbers, e-mail addresses, etc can be stored in the address book
- the receptionist may access electronic diaries to confirm visitors' appointments

Below is an illustration from a desktop information management application called Microsoft Outlook. This application not only provides an electronic diary but also allows the user to prepare 'to do' lists, make notes and send and receive messages.

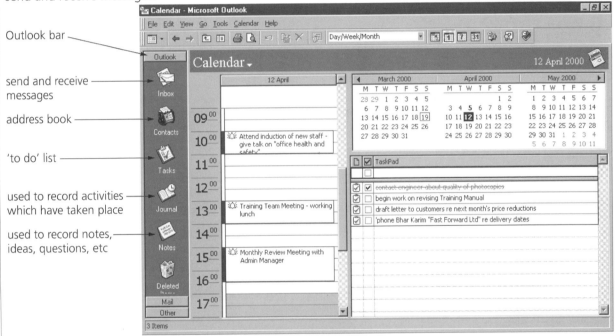

Which phone services/facilities might a receptionist use?

- Operator Services (if help is needed in making a phone call)
- Directory Enquiries (used to find a phone number or code when a directory is not available)
- caller display (shows the phone number of the caller)
- call return (used to find out the phone number of the last caller)
- frequently-called phone numbers (numbers are stored in the phone's memory and called by pressing one or two buttons)
- last number redial (last number called is redialled by pressing a button)
- charge advice (when a person making a phone call wishes to know the cost of the call)
- reverse charge (collect) call (the cost of the call is charged to the account of the person being called)

What is a mobile phone?

- hand-portable (powered by a rechargeable battery – indicator shows level of power in battery)
- operates through cellular phone system (eg Vodafone, BT Cellnet, Orange, T-Mobile)
- user may have to key in a security code before dialling the phone number required
- numbers and text shown on liquid crystal display (LCD) screen

Uses
- used to contact people who are on the move (eg visiting customers/clients)
- person can use the phone whilst away from base or whilst travelling
- important messages, eg notice of cancelled meeting, can be passed on easily and quickly to the appropriate person

Advantages	Disadvantages
<ul><li>easily transportable – modern phones are small and lightweight</li><li>easy to use</li><li>no need to get access to a public phone</li><li>person is immediately contactable provided their phone is switched on</li><li>offers extra security to person travelling alone</li><li>emergency services can be contacted quickly, eg if car breaks down</li><li>can be used to contact person almost anywhere within UK</li><li>may be used to make and receive phone calls in many countries throughout the world</li></ul>	<ul><li>calls made to or from a mobile phone are charged at a higher rate than other calls – prices are, however, becoming more competitive</li><li>phone ringing may disrupt meetings and conferences</li><li>use of a mobile phone may annoy other people, eg fellow travellers</li><li>not allowed to be used on aircraft</li><li>it is illegal to use a hand-held phone whilst driving (adaptors for hands-free use are available)</li><li>person may have her/his work continually interrupted by phone calls</li></ul>

Other facilities may include:
- voicemail
- receipt and transmission of text messages
- access to the Internet through WAP (Wireless Application Protocol) technology.

What is a pager?

- used to contact people who often work away from their office or who may have to be contacted outwith the normal working day
- if pager sounds then person knows that they need to call their base immediately (some pagers have different tones to indicate different messages)
- display-type pagers provide more information, eg the phone number to be called and a brief message
- the cost of using the pager depends on the area/zone in which it is being used

What security procedures should be followed by organisations?

The reception area will usually be located near to the main entrance. Other entrances should be safeguarded, eg by requiring the keying in of a code number known only to employees or the swiping of a security card/pass to unlock the door.

On entering the building at the start of the day, staff may be required to enter information in a Staff Signing-in Book. All members of staff should be required to wear an identification badge, preferably with a photograph, at all times. When leaving and returning to the building during the day, staff should enter information in a Staff In/Out Book.

A visitor to an organisation should be required to report to reception to check her/his appointment, enter appropriate information (name, time of arrival, company name, name of person to be seen, car registration number, etc) in a Visitors' Book and be issued with a security badge. The visitor must enter her/his time of departure in the Visitors' Book and return her/his security badge when leaving the organisation.

Visitors should be taken or directed to the room where they are to be seen or directed to a waiting area from where they will be collected. The access of visitors to areas of the building where important or sensitive information is dealt with should be strictly limited. If access to these areas is required then visitors must be supervised at all times.

What security procedures should be followed at the reception area?

- there should always be a member of staff at reception – another member of staff should be available to take over at lunch/coffee breaks and when the receptionist is absent
- the receptionist must make sure that all visitor records are completed fully and accurately
- the receptionist should not take part in confidential phone conversations in front of visitors
- any paperwork which the receptionist is dealing with must be kept out of view of visitors
- the receptionist's computer screen should be angled away from the view of visitors
- filing cabinets in the reception area should be locked when the reception area has to be left unattended; computers should be shut down

What type of security measures may an organisation use?

Security measure	Features
CCTV	• cameras placed at key viewing points inside and outside building • cameras may rotate and be capable of scanning wide areas • monitors can be viewed by staff responsible for security (reception staff, gatekeepers, etc) • recordings may be made on videotape • staff may be able to control the direction of cameras remotely and adjust the focus of cameras so as to provide better identification, record car number plates, etc
Locked doors	• doors are kept locked – doors are unlocked by a member of staff when other members of staff or authorised visitors wish to enter
Keypad/Combination locks	• numbered keypad fitted on outside door/wall of staff entrances or on door/wall of secure room within the building • a security entry number, made known only to members of staff, has to be keyed in before the door will open • keypads will not operate when the organisation is closed • doors with keypads must not be left propped open
Entryphone	• entrance doors are kept locked • a notice invites visitor to press a buzzer and provide information into a microphone system • the receptionist listens to visitor's information and remotely opens door catch as appropriate
Swipe card	• members of staff are issued with a plastic card which must be swiped through a device to unlock the door and gain access to the building or to certain rooms within the building • the magnetic strip on the swipe card contains a security code • staff must keep swipe cards secure
Security/ID badges	• staff are issued with security/ID badges • badges give the name of the member of staff, her/his position and section/department within the organisation • the badge will usually contain a photograph • security/ID badges may have to be shown to security personnel on entry
Appointments Book, Visitors' Book, Staff In/Out Book	• provide information on appointments and records of visitors and staff entering and leaving the premises
Visitor badges	• given to authorised visitors by staff at reception • authorised visitors can be identified quickly by members of staff
Security personnel (security guards, gatekeepers, etc)	• may provide an initial security check on visitors and staff entering and leaving the premises/ car park – security personnel will usually be located beside the main entrance • in some organisations, security staff may be required to search briefcases and bags • security personnel may be called upon to deal with unauthorised or aggressive visitors

How should security problems be dealt with in an organisation?

Security Problem	Procedure
Suspicious parcel left at reception	• attempt to identify the person/organisation who delivered the parcel and who the parcel is for – do not attempt to move the parcel • inform security personnel • if still concerned, evacuate the reception area and call the police • enter information on an Incident/Security Breach Report Form or in an Incident Book
Aggressive visitor	• try to calm the visitor by talking to her/him – do not attempt to restrain the visitor • if visitor still aggressive, call security personnel to escort the visitor from the premises • the visitor's organisation may be informed about the visitor's behaviour • enter information on an Incident/Security Breach Report Form or in an Incident Book
Unauthorised person gaining access to the premises	• try to find out the location of the unauthorised visitor • call security personnel • call police as appropriate • enter information on an Incident/Security Breach Report Form or in an Incident Book
Abandoned car in car park	• call security personnel • inform police if unable to trace owner • enter information on an Incident/Security Breach Report Form or in an Incident Book

INCIDENT/SECURITY BREACH REPORT FORM

Name of Person Reporting Incident	Jenny Kerr
Position in Organisation	Receptionist
Date and Time of Incident	12 May 2000, 2.35 pm
Place Where Incident Occurred	Reception
Names of Other Witnesses	Sam Ryan
Description of Incident	Mr Fairgrieve, a sales representative from Quentin Designs, became very angry when informed that there was no one available to see him. I could not reason with Mr Fairgrieve so I called Sam Ryan for assistance.
Action Taken at the Time	Sam talked to Mr Fairgrieve and managed to calm him down. He agreed that he had over-reacted and apologised for his behaviour.
Further Action Required	Sam is to inform the Sales Manager of Quentin Designs of the incident.
Signature of Line Manager	Sam Ryan
Date	15 May 2000

What records are kept at reception?

Staff Signing-In Book

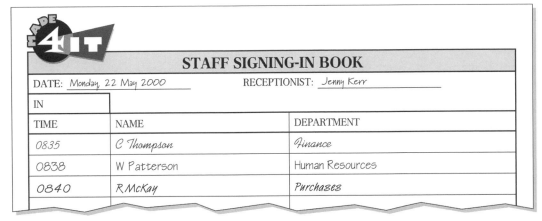

STAFF SIGNING-IN BOOK

DATE: Monday, 22 May 2000   RECEPTIONIST: Jenny Kerr

IN

TIME	NAME	DEPARTMENT
0835	C Thompson	Finance
0838	W Patterson	Human Resources
0840	R McKay	Purchases

Staff In/Out Book

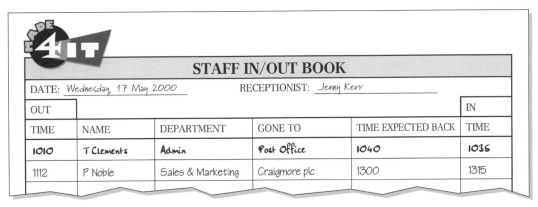

STAFF IN/OUT BOOK

DATE: Wednesday, 17 May 2000   RECEPTIONIST: Jenny Kerr

OUT | | | | | IN

TIME	NAME	DEPARTMENT	GONE TO	TIME EXPECTED BACK	TIME
1010	T Clements	Admin	Post Office	1040	1035
1112	P Noble	Sales & Marketing	Craigmore plc	1300	1315

Appointments Book

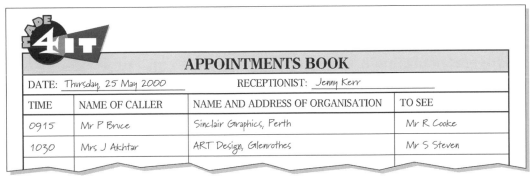

APPOINTMENTS BOOK

DATE: Thursday, 25 May 2000   RECEPTIONIST: Jenny Kerr

TIME	NAME OF CALLER	NAME AND ADDRESS OF ORGANISATION	TO SEE
0915	Mr P Bruce	Sinclair Graphics, Perth	Mr R Cooke
1030	Mrs J Akhtar	ART Design, Glenrothes	Mr S Steven

Visitors' Book

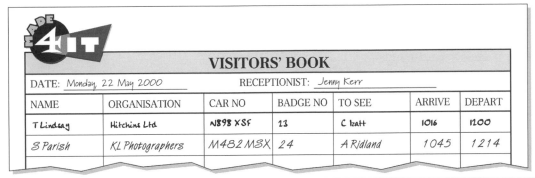

VISITORS' BOOK

DATE: Monday, 22 May 2000   RECEPTIONIST: Jenny Kerr

NAME	ORGANISATION	CAR NO	BADGE NO	TO SEE	ARRIVE	DEPART
T Lindsay	Hitchins Ltd	N898 XSF	13	C Izatt	1016	1200
S Parish	KL Photographers	M482 MSX	24	A Ridland	1045	1214

2d The Working Environment: Mail Handling

How do businesses communicate information?

internal mail – memos, reports, notices, forms, etc sent between employees working for the same organisation by internal e-mail or collected and distributed within the organisation by the organisation's own messenger service

external mail – letters, reports, forms, publicity materials, etc sent outwith the organisation by the Royal Mail postal service, fax, external e-mail or by an external courier service

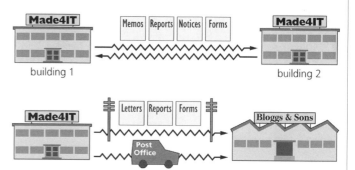

building 1   building 2

What is electronic mail (e-mail)?

- messages are sent from one computer to another through a system of 'mailboxes' (a message may be sent at the same time to a number of different mailboxes)
- e-mail may be internal (sent between networked computers within the same organisation) or external (sent between computers which are connected using the phone system)
- member of staff accesses her/his mailbox by using a password and/or ID
- a list of frequently-used e-mail addresses can be stored on the computer in an address book – saves time and avoids errors in keying in addresses

> **Internal e-mail** = messages passed within an organisation from one computer to another using e-mail software and the organisation's own computer network
>
> **External e-mail** = messages passed from one computer to another using an external e-mail service or the Internet and the phone system to link the computers

What is the procedure for handling internal mail?

- internal mail should be collected from employees' out-trays at regular intervals throughout the day
- documents should state clearly the date, the name and position of the sender and the name and position of the receiver – this information may be shown on a compliments slip attached to the document or may be shown in the headings to the document, eg the headings to a memo
- some organisations use internal transit envelopes for sending documents within the organisation – the sender enters the name, department and location of the receiver on the front of the envelope, making sure to cancel any previous internal address
- private/personal/confidential internal mail should be sealed in an envelope with the name of the receiver and the word 'confidential' clearly marked on the outside
- where a document has to be seen by a number of people, photocopies should be made of the document or a circulation/routing slip attached to the document
- urgent internal mail should be delivered immediately
- internal mail should be sorted using trays, pigeon holes, etc and then delivered to the appropriate person/department
- where an organisation has its own messenger/courier service to collect and take internal mail from one area to another or from one building to another then uplift deadline times should be known to staff throughout the organisation

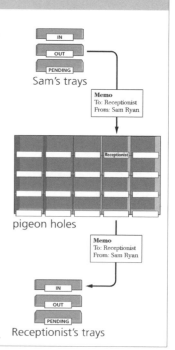

Sam's trays

pigeon holes

Receptionist's trays

What is the procedure for handling incoming mail?

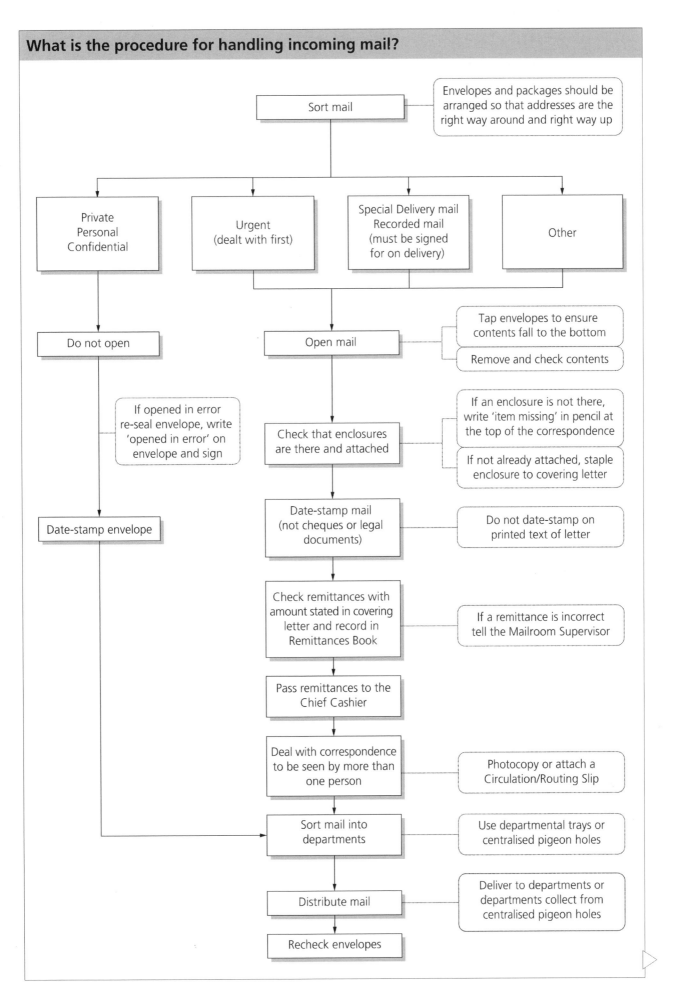

Sort mail — Envelopes and packages should be arranged so that addresses are the right way around and right way up

Branches:
- **Private Personal Confidential**
- **Urgent (dealt with first)**
- **Special Delivery mail Recorded mail (must be signed for on delivery)**
- **Other**

Private Personal Confidential → **Do not open**
- If opened in error re-seal envelope, write 'opened in error' on envelope and sign
- → **Date-stamp envelope**

Open mail
- Tap envelopes to ensure contents fall to the bottom
- Remove and check contents

Check that enclosures are there and attached
- If an enclosure is not there, write 'item missing' in pencil at the top of the correspondence
- If not already attached, staple enclosure to covering letter

Date-stamp mail (not cheques or legal documents)
- Do not date-stamp on printed text of letter

Check remittances with amount stated in covering letter and record in Remittances Book
- If a remittance is incorrect tell the Mailroom Supervisor

Pass remittances to the Chief Cashier

Deal with correspondence to be seen by more than one person
- Photocopy or attach a Circulation/Routing Slip

Sort mail into departments
- Use departmental trays or centralised pigeon holes

Distribute mail
- Deliver to departments or departments collect from centralised pigeon holes

Recheck envelopes

What is the procedure for handling incoming mail? (cont.)

Some organisations scan all documents received in the mail into their computer system. The scanner converts a document into a digital form and saves it as a file on the computer.

> **Scanning** = inputting source material (printed text, drawings, photographs, etc) on to computer file for storage, manipulation or insertion into other documents

The procedure followed by mailroom staff would be as follows:

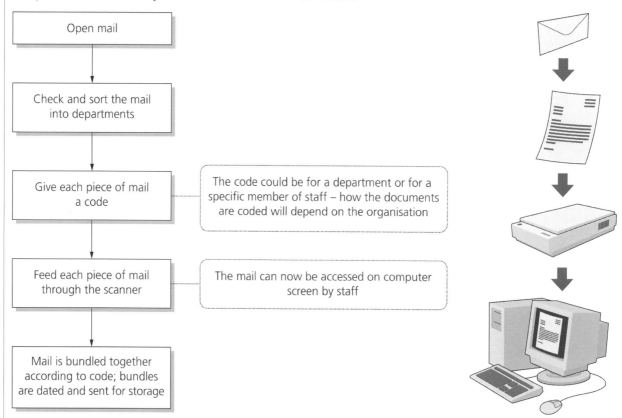

```
Open mail
   │
   ▼
Check and sort the mail
into departments
   │
   ▼
Give each piece of mail ┄┄┄ The code could be for a department or for a
a code                       specific member of staff – how the documents
   │                         are coded will depend on the organisation
   ▼
Feed each piece of mail ┄┄┄ The mail can now be accessed on computer
through the scanner          screen by staff
   │
   ▼
Mail is bundled together
according to code; bundles
are dated and sent for storage
```

When staff log on to the computer system they see a list of all mail that has been received that day. Staff then select a piece of mail to deal with by clicking and opening it. If there is a need to refer to other documents, eg previous correspondence, then these can be retrieved and looked at on screen. Any replies that have to be made can be keyed in and saved using the organisation's coding system.

What is the procedure for handling incoming e-mail messages?

- where an employee is unable to check her/his own electronic mailbox then she/he should arrange for another employee to do so and to deal with any messages – it is possible for an employee to check her/his electronic mailbox even when away from the premises by using a laptop computer and phone link
- electronic mailboxes should be checked on a regular basis throughout the day
- urgent e-mail must be dealt with quickly (where an employee is away from the office and cannot access her/his own electronic mailbox, urgent messages should be printed and drawn to the attention of the employee concerned or faxed/e-mailed to the employee's location)
- e-mail which should be seen by a number of employees should be routed or copied to the employees concerned

What is the procedure for handling outgoing mail?

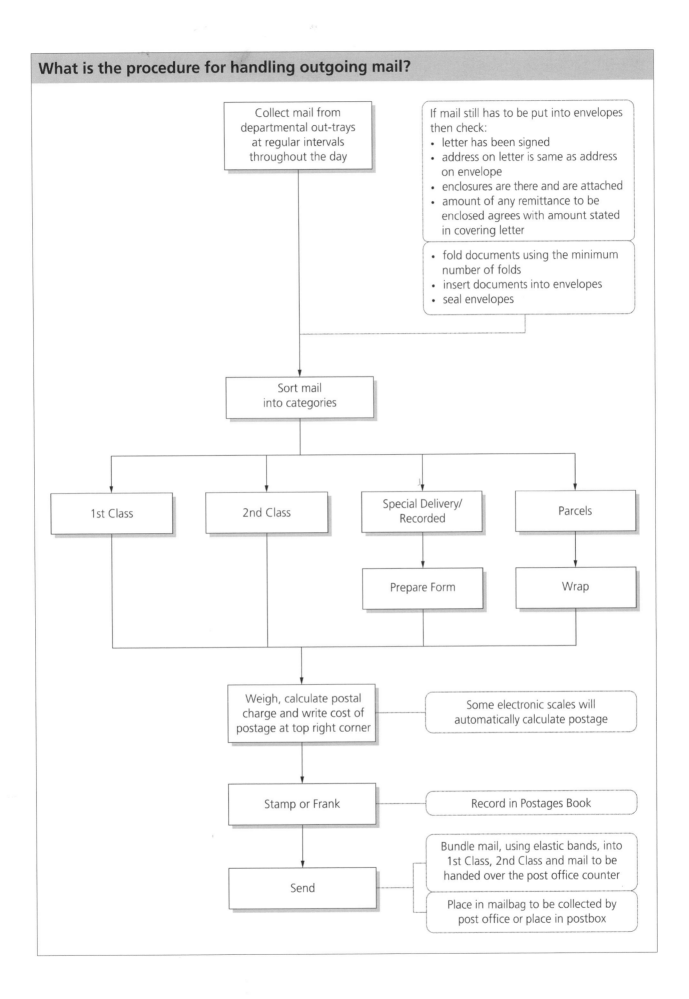

Collect mail from departmental out-trays at regular intervals throughout the day

If mail still has to be put into envelopes then check:
- letter has been signed
- address on letter is same as address on envelope
- enclosures are there and are attached
- amount of any remittance to be enclosed agrees with amount stated in covering letter

- fold documents using the minimum number of folds
- insert documents into envelopes
- seal envelopes

Sort mail into categories

1st Class

2nd Class

Special Delivery/ Recorded

Parcels

Prepare Form

Wrap

Weigh, calculate postal charge and write cost of postage at top right corner

Some electronic scales will automatically calculate postage

Stamp or Frank

Record in Postages Book

Send

Bundle mail, using elastic bands, into 1st Class, 2nd Class and mail to be handed over the post office counter

Place in mailbag to be collected by post office or place in postbox

What is voicemail?

- if person being phoned is not available to answer a call then a prerecorded message invites the caller to leave a message
- to listen to any voicemail messages, user dials her/his voicemail box – may require the use of a Personal Identification Number (PIN)
- voicemail messages can also be received or sent by computer (computer must have software and a microphone installed)

Uses

- to receive calls when the organisation is closed
- to leave messages for people who are away from their workstation or have their mobile phone switched off

Advantages	*Disadvantages*
• allows messages to be left for a person who is not available to receive a phone call – callers feel that they are being dealt with • allows calls to be received 24 hours a day • avoids errors being made by someone else passing on messages verbally or in writing • messages can be listened to at a convenient time	• person required may not check voicemail on a regular basis • no opportunity to seek clarification or further information from caller • some people may not like to leave verbal messages

What is fax?

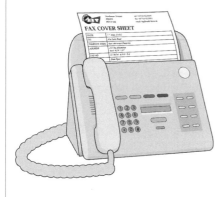

- exact (facsimile) copies of documents containing text, graphics or photographs can be sent easily and at very high speed over phone lines to almost anywhere in the world
- cost depends on the time of day, distance and duration of the transmission
- less expensive fax machines use coated, heat-sensitive (thermal) paper; more expensive plain paper fax machines may also be used as plain paper photocopiers
- all fax machines can transmit and receive messages
- frequently-dialled numbers can be stored in the fax machine's memory
- a transmission report can be printed to confirm transmission and show the length and time of transmission
- most organisations have a separate dedicated phone line for receiving and sending faxes

What is the procedure for dealing with faxes?

- outgoing faxes should be given to a designated member of staff (possibly the receptionist) for transmission – that person should check that all necessary information has been entered on the **Fax Cover Sheet** (see page 47)
- a transmission report should be printed to confirm successful transmission of the outgoing fax (the transmission report should be attached to the original message and passed back to the sender) – some fax machines produce a summary transmission report which provides information on a number of the most recent outgoing faxes

- where fax machines are left unattended they must be checked for incoming faxes on a regular basis throughout the day, eg at the beginning of the day and at hourly intervals thereafter
- the number of pages of an incoming fax should be checked against the number shown on the incoming Fax Cover Sheet – if part of a message is missing then the sender should be contacted and asked to send the fax again
- the pages of an incoming fax should be stapled together
- all incoming faxes should be passed on quickly (urgent faxes should be drawn to the attention of the employees concerned – not left in an in-tray or on a desk)

What is the procedure for dealing with faxes? (cont.)

10 Newhouse Avenue

PERTH

PH12 6XJ

tel: 01738 622656

fax: 01738 622661

email: hq@made4it.co.uk

FAX COVER SHEET

DATE	11 May 2000
TO	Ms Katie Blair
COMPANY NAME	York Universal Supplies
ADDRESS	24 The Shambles York YO4 1BT
FAX NO	01904 479132
FROM	Sam Ryan
MESSAGE	Please note that Order No 4871670 which was sent to you yesterday contained an error. Instead of 2000 double-sided high-density 1.44MB formatted floppy disks only 200 are required. Please cancel the complete order. A replacement order has been sent to you today by first class post.

NO OF PAGES INCLUDING COVER SHEET: 1

What are the advantages and disadvantages of using e-mail and fax?

Advantages	*Disadvantages*
• messages are sent at very high speed • graphics, illustrations, etc can be sent just as easily as text • lengthy messages (word-processed documents, spreadsheets, etc) can be prepared separately and sent as attachments to e-mail messages at low-cost transmission times • messages can be sent at any time to anywhere in the world • e-mail and fax are comparatively low cost – the main cost is the transmission charge for using the phone link • a printout can easily be made of e-mail messages to provide a permanent record or e-mail messages can be saved as text files on a hard disk (a fax is its own permanent record) • e-mail messages can be filed, deleted, replied to, forwarded to another person or sent to a group of people • security of e-mail messages may be improved by using passwords to restrict access to mailboxes or by using encryption software when sending messages • fax machines are relatively inexpensive – fax machines may incorporate phone, telephone-answering and photocopying facilities	• when wishing to send an e-mail over the Internet there may be problems in getting through to the Internet Service Provider (ISP) or there may be a breakdown in the link with the ISP or the computer system may temporarily fail • the sender has to know the e-mail address or the fax number of the recipient • there is no automatic confirmation that a fax has been received by the intended recipient • there is no automatic indication that e-mail messages have been received and opened • fax machines will only accept A4 or smaller documents • if the quality of the faxed document is poor then the receiver may find it difficult to read the fax • an organisation is likely to require a separate dedicated phone line for sending and receiving faxes • there may be a time delay in recipients checking their mailboxes and reading any new messages • faxed documents would not usually be accepted as legally-binding documents

What machines/equipment are used in the mailroom?

Electronic Postal Scales

- weighs a package and automatically calculates the postal charge (weight and price displayed)
- more sophisticated electronic machines can be used for weighing and calculating the cost of inland letters and parcels (including Special Delivery and Recorded), European mail and overseas air and surface mail
- changes in postal rates may be made via the keyboard or by inserting a new 'chip' in the machine

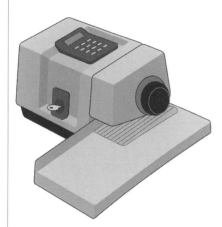

Franking Machine
- prints postal impression (postal charge, date and place of posting) on to envelopes or labels
- faster than sticking stamps on to envelopes
- avoids having to purchase stamps (less chance of theft)
- postal impression can also include an advertising slogan
- machine may be purchased, leased or rented from manufacturers
- units of postage purchased in advance from post office
- additional units are purchased by taking part of the machine (module) to the post office and getting it credited with additional units or by purchasing additional units over a direct phone link

direct phone link
module

Date Stamp
- used to stamp the date of receipt on incoming mail
- current date is set at the beginning of each day
- date of receipt may be referred to if there is a query about when an item of mail was received or the time taken to deal with a piece of correspondence
- date is stamped on a blank area of the correspondence – not over the text

What would influence the method chosen for sending different types of internal and external mail?

- urgency (how quickly is the information required?)
- size (what is the length of the document?)
- need for confidentiality (does the document contain private or sensitive information?)
- value of the information (would the organisation wish compensation if the item was lost or stolen?)
- method used by the organisation to send similar information in the past
- methods of communication available to the organisation and their costs
- relationship between the sender and the receiver (are they well known to each other?)
- status/position of the person the message is being sent to
- ICT hardware and software available to the sender and the receiver
- need for the receiver to have the information in writing or to have a copy of original document

How should different types of communication be sent?

Example of type of communication	Internal/ External mail	Suggested method(s)	Reason for choosing method(s)
A letter to a new customer inviting her/him to a sales exhibition	External	Royal Mail (first/second class)	• sender wishes to create a good impression • sender and receiver will not be known to each other • whether sent first or second class will depend on the urgency of the communication • cost is not important
An urgent letter to a supplier cancelling an order	External	Fax (marked 'urgent') and follow-up letter by Royal Mail postal service (first class)	• need to send information quickly • need for supplier to be provided with accurate, detailed information in writing in case of possible dispute • cost is not important – fax and letter
A message to a group of employees cancelling a meeting next week	Internal	E-mail or memo	• e-mail likely to be chosen where already in widespread use within the organisation • need to send information reasonably quickly
A message outwith office hours to inform another organisation that a sales representative will not be able to make an important meeting with them the following morning	External	E-mail or fax or voicemail or message left on telephone answering machine (indicate urgency)	• need to send information quickly • no need for formality – the message is more important than the style
An urgent press statement to local newspapers concerning possible large-scale redundancies within the organisation	External	Fax (marked urgent)	• need to send information quickly • need for press to be provided with accurate, detailed information in writing
Details of the organisation's latest profit figures which must be sent urgently to HQ for discussion at a Board Meeting	Internal	Secure e-mail (use of encryption and passwords)	• need to send information quickly • need to have accurate, detailed information • need to keep information secure
A legal document which is required urgently by the organisation's solicitors	External	Royal Mail postal service (Special Delivery) or courier service	• need to send information quickly • need to safeguard document during transit • need for compensation in the event of loss of the document
A copy of a long company report which requires to be sent to Germany for a meeting the following day	External	E-mail with report as an attachment	• need to send information quickly • need for accurate, detailed information • need for information in writing • report can be scanned or keyed in prior to e-mail being sent • low cost • report can be printed and copies made as required

3a Storage and Retrieval of Information: Purpose of Filing

What is the purpose of filing?

- so that documents can be found quickly and easily
- so that information is readily available to answer queries
- so that up-to-date information can be provided when required
- to keep documents secure – especially those containing sensitive or confidential information
- to keep documents clean and tidy, and protect them from wear and tear
- to satisfy legal requirements (eg legal contracts, bank statements and tax forms have to be kept for a minimum number of years)

What are the features of a good filing system?

- simple and quick to use
- conveniently located
- appropriate for the type of information held
- economical in the use of floor space
- relatively inexpensive to install and maintain
- flexible (to meet changes in the volume or type of information held)
- easy to monitor and control (it should be easy to check and remove old documents)
- secure (only authorised staff should be able to access the system)
- safe (it should protect documents from fire, flood and wear and tear)

What filing procedures are used by organisations?

- documents should be filed daily – usually towards the end of each day
- documents should be checked to make sure that they have been released for filing – a release mark could be:
  - the letter 'F' for file
  - a tick
  - an employee's initials
  - the word 'File' at the top right of the papers
  - a line drawn across the papers

- documents should be sorted into order (alphabetical or numerical) before they are placed in the filing system
- papers which have to be kept together should be stapled (paperclips should be removed as they may catch on other documents)
- a numerical file reference should be written on documents as appropriate
- documents within a file should be arranged in chronological order (date order) with the most recent document placed at the front of the file
- 'absent markers'/'out guides'/'absent folders' should be used when papers/files are borrowed
- 'cross-reference' cards/sheets should be used when a file could be placed in more than one place within the filing system
- confidential documents/files should be kept in a separate lockable filing cabinet
- old papers/files should be removed on a regular basis – the organisation will usually have agreed retention periods (ie the length of time papers should be kept in active files before being placed in transfer files and then into dead files – legal documents will have a longer retention period than normal correspondence)

3b Storage and Retrieval of Information: Methods

What are the features, advantages and disadvantages of alphabetical, numerical and chronological methods of filing?

Method and Features	Advantages	Disadvantages
Alphabetical • customers' folders are arranged in alphabetical order • guide cards or tabs (showing each letter of the alphabet or subdivisions of common letters) may be used to speed up finding a file A – D	• straightforward form of filing – easy to understand and use • direct reference method of filing – does not require the use of an index • suitable for small- to medium-sized organisations • a miscellaneous file/folder can be kept at the beginning or end of each letter of the alphabet to store correspondence from customers who do not write frequently	• requires a thorough knowledge of the alphabetical filing rules used by the organisation • not suitable for large organisations with many customers • may be slow to find a file especially where many customers have the same surname • can be wasteful of space within cabinet drawers – some letters of the alphabet (eg 'M') require a lot of space and others (eg 'Q') very little • if extra space is required for a particular letter of the alphabet then the system may require considerable rearrangement
Numerical • files are arranged in numerical order • a new customer is given the next number (added to the end of the files) 50 – 64	• suitable for large organisations • suitable for organisations where it is useful to have a reference number allocated to each customer (the number can be used as a reference on all correspondence) • files are less likely to be misplaced in the filing system • easily expanded (provided that additional filing cabinets are available) • alphabetical index can be used for finding other information, eg addresses and phone numbers of customers	• indirect method of filing (requires the preparation and use of an alphabetical index to find a customer's file number) • the alphabetical index needs to be constantly updated for new customers • difficult to provide for miscellaneous files/folders
Chronological • documents are filed in chronological order (date order) • usual method of arranging papers within files when using other methods (eg alphabetical and numerical) – the most recent documents would be placed at the front of files 2000 – 2001	• may be suitable for organisations or sections within organisations where dates are the key feature of the information to be filed • may be used along with another method of filing, eg application forms may be filed alphabetically with copies of the forms being filed according to the year/month received	• unlikely to be used as the main method of filing • without some form of index it would be very difficult to remember when a document was sent/received and to retrieve the document from the filing system

What are the features, advantages and disadvantages of manual and electronic filing?

System and Features	Advantages	Disadvantages
Manual • original documents are stored in concertina files, box files or filing cabinets (vertical, lateral or plan) • sorters may be used to pre-sort documents before they are placed in filing cabinets	• the system is likely to be familiar to staff – little training is likely to be required to use the equipment • metal filing cabinets give some protection to documents against fire and flood, and wear and tear • metal filing cabinets will last a long time • people often prefer reading original documents • the drawers of filing cabinets will usually be clearly labelled and tabs placed on pockets so as to speed up finding a file	• metal filing cabinets are relatively expensive • accidents may happen if filing cabinets are not used properly (eg drawers left open) • may be difficult to locate a document quickly in large manual filing systems • boxes or cabinets may soon become overloaded • may take some time to go through files and weed out old documents • if the original document is lost or stolen it is unlikely that the organisation will have a back up copy
Electronic (computerised) • documents produced on individual computers are sent via a network for central storage on disk/tape/CD-ROM • documents received by the organisation are scanned into the computerised filing system using a document scanner • software applications, eg word processing or spreadsheet, use computerised filing systems with each document being given a title and filed in a folder on disk	• saves filing space (thousands of documents can be stored on one disk/tape/CD-ROM) • documents can be scanned in quickly and easily • documents/information can be found quickly using search criteria, eg date or key words • the same document can be accessed by others in the organisation from their own computers – avoids duplication of information • a vast amount of information can be made available to staff • computerised databases can be queried, sorted and reports prepared quickly and easily • security codes can be used to restrict access to confidential documents • the contents of folders can be viewed/scrolled quickly prior to selecting a particular document • back up files can be easily prepared	• unlikely to be appropriate for very small organisations • training in the use of computerised system will be required • faults in the power supply, computer system or computer network may mean that it is temporarily not possible to retrieve information from files • organisations will have to comply with the requirements of the Data Protection Act

What is file management?

File management is the way in which computer data is stored and organised.

The operating system of the computer allows the user to store, delete, rename, move or copy files. The operating system records the location, length, and date and time of creation of each file.

Whenever data is saved, it is saved in a file. Every file must be given an appropriate name so that it can be identified and, if necessary, retrieved at a later date.

When a file is saved, some operating systems automatically give the filename an extension, ie after the filename it inserts a full stop followed by three letters. The extension allows the computer to identify the type of file, ie the software application used to create the file.

The following are the most common file extensions:
- a file created in Microsoft Word would have .doc as its extension – if the file was named 'Brown Quote1' the computer would save it as 'Brown Quote1.doc'
- a file created in Microsoft Excel would have .xls as its extension – if the file was named 'Cash Budget March' the computer would save it as 'Cash Budget March.xls'
- a file created in Microsoft Access would have .mdb as its extension – if the file was named 'Employees' the computer would save it as 'Employees.mdb'
- a graphics file would be given an extension depending on what type of graphic it was, eg .bmp or .pcx – if the file was named 'Logo' it might be saved as 'Logo.bmp'.

Sometimes the computer system will show the filename but not the file extension. This does not mean that the filename does not have an extension – it just means that the computer system has hidden the file extension.

To enable files to be found easily an organisation may arrange its electronic filing system so that similar files, ie those created in the same application, are stored together in a folder (a folder is sometimes called a directory).

How an organisation arranges its files in folders will depend on the needs of the organisation. Made4IT could have the following file structure:

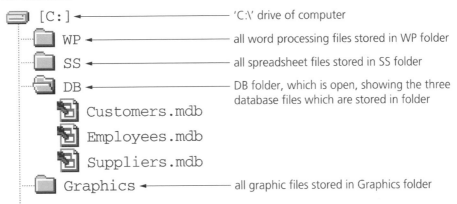

- [C:] ———————— 'C:\' drive of computer
- WP ———————— all word processing files stored in WP folder
- SS ———————— all spreadsheet files stored in SS folder
- DB ———————— DB folder, which is open, showing the three database files which are stored in folder
  - Customers.mdb
  - Employees.mdb
  - Suppliers.mdb
- Graphics ———————— all graphic files stored in Graphics folder

What is a database?

A database is a collection of related information. A database can be:
- paper-based, eg phone book, card index of customers' information or list of internal phone extension numbers
- electronic (computerised), eg details of staff, customers or suppliers.

Computerised database = a structured collection of related data (eg names, addresses, phone numbers and credit limits of customers) held in a computer file

What are the advantages of using a computerised database?

- records of customers, suppliers, employees, etc can be added/deleted/edited quickly and easily
- data can be searched quickly and easily to locate specific pieces of data
- data can be sorted quickly and easily in different ways to suit the needs of the organisation
- if the database is kept on an intranet, it can be accessed by a number of employees at the same time
- access to the database can be restricted to certain employees
- there are no record cards to wear out or become damaged

What is the structure of a computerised database?

A Table (Datasheet)
(These terms apply to Microsoft Access – other database applications may use different terminologies.)
Below is an extract of a table containing data relating to the customers of Made4IT. The table is set out in rows and columns.

field names

Company Name	Address	Town	Postcode	Phone No	Contact Name
Arts and Media	44 High Street	DALKEITH	EH22 4TR	0131 663 3443	Mr Mike Copland
Fast Forward Ltd	84 Bertram Road	GLASGOW	G64 1TX	0141 762 1899	Mr Bhar Karim
Dundee Security Ltd	44 The Shore	DUNDEE	DD5 1BB	01382 732965	Mrs Rosie Hakim
Moffat, David & Sons	93 Main Street	PERTH	PH1 4DZ	01738 560000	Miss Laura Gregor
Brown Brothers	120 Ward Street	EDINBURGH	EH8 3AD	0131 667 0433	Ms Katie Foley
Border PC Services	16 Old Town	PEEBLES	EH45 9DE	01721 721198	Mr Nicholas Briggs
Wedding Shop The	342 Waterloo Place	CHELMSFORD	CM1 1GY	01245 493393	Ms Elizabeth Nauman
PG Computers plc	3 Port Way	PORTSMOUTH	PO6 4TT	01705 243855	Ms Ellie Snowdon
De Luxe Printers	132 London Street	READING	RG1 4DQ	01734 765391	Mr Ian Johnson
P & J Insurance Co	23 King Street	ABERDEEN	AB21 1PS	01224 644446	Ms Kate Archibald
Struan Windows	44 Robert Avenue	EDINBURGH	EH1 4AZ	0131 225 6543	Mr Miles Wylie
Eskbank Design Co	14 Newbattle Road	DALKEITH	EH22 4AZ	0131 663 3456	Miss Lynette Brown

records
(each row is
a record)

fields (each column is a field)

Data = any information (text, numbers, etc) which is entered in a table

How are changes made to a database?

Changing Data in a Table
The records in a table can be added to, deleted or edited:
- adding records to a table means keying in a new record, eg keying in the data for a new customer
- deleting records from a table means permanently removing records, eg removing the record of an ex-customer
- editing records in a table means altering the data, eg changing a customer's phone number (adding or deleting records can also be looked upon as editing).

Formatting Data in a Table
Data in a field may be formatted (displayed) in different ways, eg a field may be formatted to show dates as 03/05/00 or as 3 May 2000. Similarly, numbers in a field may be formatted as whole numbers or as numbers with decimal places.

Finding Data in a Table
A database operator can search a single field or a number of fields to locate specific data. This is done by using the '**Find**' facility. If the operator asks the database to find the record that contains the Contact Name 'Mrs Rosie Hakim' then the name Mrs Rosie Hakim will be highlighted if the database finds the information.

Company Name	Address	Town	Postcode	Phone No	Contact Name
Arts and Media	44 High Street	DALKEITH	EH22 4TR	0131 663 3443	Mr Mike Copland
Fast Forward Ltd	84 Bertram Road	GLASGOW	G64 1TX	0141 762 1899	Mr Bhar Karim
Dundee Security Ltd	44 The Shore	DUNDEE	DD5 1BB	01382 732965	**Mrs Rosie Hakim**
Moffat, David & Sons	93 Main Street	PERTH	PH1 4DZ	01738 560000	Miss Laura Gregor

Another way of finding information is by using the '**Filter**' facility. If the operator asks the database to find all the records that contain the Town EDINBURGH then all records with the town EDINBURGH will be shown on screen (all other records will be hidden).

Company Name	Address	Town	Postcode	Phone No	Contact Name
Brown Brothers	120 Ward Street	EDINBURGH	EH8 3AD	0131 667 0433	Ms Katie Foley
Struan Windows	44 Robert Avenue	EDINBURGH	EH1 4AZ	0131 225 6543	Mr Miles Wylie

Sorting Data in a Table

The data in a table can be sorted, using the '**Sort**' facility, into ascending or descending order, eg the operator might ask the database to sort the data so that the towns appear in ascending order (starting with towns beginning with the letter 'A', then 'B' and so on).

Company Name	Address	Town	Postcode	Phone No	Contact Name
P & J Insurance Co	23 King Street	ABERDEEN	AB21 1PS	01224 644446	Ms Kate Archibald
Wedding Shop The	342 Waterloo Place	CHELMSFORD	CM1 1GY	01245 493393	Ms Elizabeth Nauman
Arts and Media	44 High Street	DALKEITH	EH22 4TR	0131 663 3443	Mr Mike Copland
Eskbank Design Co	14 Newbattle Road	DALKEITH	EH22 4AZ	0131 663 3456	Miss Lynette Brown
Dundee Security Ltd	44 The Shore	DUNDEE	DD5 1BB	01382 732965	Mrs Rosie Hakim
Struan Windows	44 Robert Avenue	EDINBURGH	EH1 4AZ	0131 225 6543	Mr Miles Wylie
Brown Brothers	120 Ward Street	EDINBURGH	EH8 3AD	0131 667 0433	Ms Katie Foley
Fast Forward Ltd	84 Bertram Road	GLASGOW	G64 1TX	0141 762 1899	Mr Bhar Karim
Border PC Services	16 Old Town	PEEBLES	EH45 9DE	01721 721198	Mr Nicholas Briggs
Moffat, David & Sons	93 Main Street	PERTH	PH1 4DZ	01738 560000	Miss Laura Gregor
PG Computers plc	3 Port Way	PORTSMOUTH	PO6 4TT	01705 243855	Ms Ellie Snowdon
De Luxe Printers	132 London Street	READING	RG1 4DQ	01734 765391	Mr Ian Johnson

What is a spreadsheet?

A spreadsheet is a software application which is used to manage numbers and carry out calculations. It contains text, numbers and formulae which are keyed in on a grid of cells – set out as horizontal rows (indicated by numbers) and vertical columns (indicated by letters). A cell is the point at which a column and row intersect.

To put data into a spreadsheet, a cell must be selected (when a cell is selected it is known as the active cell) and the data keyed in and entered. Below is a spreadsheet showing sales data.

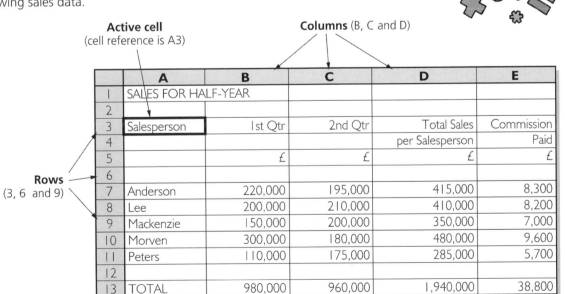

Active cell
(cell reference is A3)

Columns (B, C and D)

Rows
(3, 6 and 9)

	A	B	C	D	E
1	SALES FOR HALF-YEAR				
2					
3	Salesperson	1st Qtr	2nd Qtr	Total Sales	Commission
4				per Salesperson	Paid
5		£	£	£	£
6					
7	Anderson	220,000	195,000	415,000	8,300
8	Lee	200,000	210,000	410,000	8,200
9	Mackenzie	150,000	200,000	350,000	7,000
10	Morven	300,000	180,000	480,000	9,600
11	Peters	110,000	175,000	285,000	5,700
12					
13	TOTAL	980,000	960,000	1,940,000	38,800

What are the advantages of using a spreadsheet?

- formulae calculations (adding, subtracting, totalling, multiplying, dividing, calculating percentages, etc) are carried out almost instantaneously
- calculations are done with total accuracy
- formulae are amended automatically when the spreadsheet is amended (eg another row of data added)
- text, numbers and formulae can be copied easily and quickly across rows or down columns
- data can be organised easily and quickly by sorting or filtering
- numeric data can be displayed as graphs or charts

A business may use a spreadsheet for preparing financial statements, budgets, estimates, etc.

How are changes made to a spreadsheet?

Changing Data in a Spreadsheet

The data in a spreadsheet can be added to, deleted or edited:
- adding data means keying in data into empty cells. New rows and columns can be inserted between existing rows and columns to allow data to be added.

7	Anderson	220,000	195,000	415,000	8,300
8	Bathgate	190,000	200,000	390,000	7,800
9	Lee	200,000	210,000	410,000	8,200
10	Mackenzie	150,000	200,000	350,000	7,000
11	Morven	300,000	180,000	480,000	9,600
12	Peters	110,000	175,000	285,000	5,700

new row inserted → 8

- deleting data means permanently removing data from a single cell, range of cells, a complete row or complete column
- editing data means altering the data, eg the sales figures for a salesperson (adding or deleting data can also be looked upon as editing).

Formatting Data in a Spreadsheet

Spreadsheet data can be formatted – this facility acts in a similar way to that used in a database.

Finding Data in a Spreadsheet

Data can be found by using the 'Find' or 'Filter' facilities – they act in a similar way to those used in a database.

Sorting Data in a Spreadsheet

Spreadsheet data can be sorted using the 'Sort' facility – again this acts in a similar way to that used in a database.

Spreadsheet Formulae

To get a spreadsheet to make a calculation a formula must be inserted. A formula begins with an '=' sign (if using Microsoft Excel). The spreadsheet, showing the formulae, is given below.

	A	B	C	D	E
1	SALES FOR HALF-YEAR				
2					
3	Salesperson	1st Qtr	2nd Qtr	Total Sales	Commission
4				per Salesperson	Paid
5		£	£	£	£
6					
7	Anderson	220000	195000	=B7+C7	=D7*2%
8	Bathgate	190000	200000	=B8+C8	=D8*2%
9	Lee	200000	210000	=B9+C9	=D9*2%
10	Mackenzie	150000	200000	=B10+C10	=D10*2%
11	Morven	300000	180000	=B11+C11	=D11*2%
12	Peters	110000	175000	=B12+C12	=D12*2%
13					
14	TOTAL	=SUM(B7:B12)	=SUM(C7:C12)	=SUM(D7:D12)	=SUM(E7:E12)

How are changes made to a spreadsheet? (cont.)

Copying (or filling) Formulae

After the formula (=B7+C7) has been keyed into cell D7, it can be copied (or filled) down the column to cells D8, D9, D10, D11 and D12 by using the copy (or fill) facility.

The same applies to:
- the formula (=D7*2%) keyed into cell E7. It has been copied (or filled) down to cell E12.
- the formula (=SUM(B7:B12)) keyed into cell B14. It has been copied (or filled) across to cell E14.

Graphs

A graph can be created of the data in the spreadsheet.

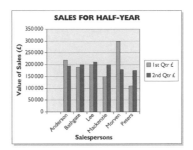

How are computer files stored?

Type of Storage	Features/Uses
Floppy Disk	3·5" HD (High Density) floppy disk – 1·44 MB storage capacity: • inexpensive and widely used – most computers have a floppy disk drive • used for temporary back up of files which are also stored on the hard drive • used to transfer documents from one computer to another Floppy disks which store up to 120 MB are available – a special drive is required to use such disks.
Zip	Zip disks – 100 or 250 MB storage capacity: • a special drive is required to use such disks • large files can be copied from the hard drive on to a zip disk
Hard Drive	The hard drives fitted in computers vary in size (currently, a typical size is 20 GB): • used for storage of applications and data
CD-ROM	CD-ROM (Compact Disc Read-Only Memory) – 650 MB storage capacity: • information can be read using a standard CD-ROM drive but cannot be edited or erased • applications software is usually supplied on CD-ROM – the software is installed from the CD-ROM on to the computer's hard drive • many sources of reference, eg newspapers, encyclopaedias and dictionaries, are available on CD-ROM • may be used to store audio, video, graphics and other large files, eg databases CD-R (Compact Disc write-once Read-many) – information can be written once to the disc but cannot be edited or erased. CD-RW (Compact Disc ReWritable) – information can be written and overwritten to this type of disc. A special drive and software are required to write to such discs.
DVD	DVD-ROM (Digital Versatile Disc Read-Only Memory) disc – 4·7, 9·4 or 17 GB storage capacity: • information can be read using a standard DVD-ROM drive but cannot be edited or erased • uses are as for CD-ROM but particularly suitable for storing sound and vision, eg feature films DVD-R (Recordable) – information can be written once to the disc but cannot be edited or erased DVD-RAM – information can be written and overwritten to this type of disc. A special drive and software are required to write to such discs.

What is microfilming?

- papers are filmed (put on microfilm) to reduce them in size (an A4 page is reduced to the size of a postage stamp)
- microfilm can be stored:
  - on rolls (a roll of film can hold thousands of documents)
  - in jackets (strips of film are kept in transparent wallets)
  - as microfiche (a sheet of film which can hold hundreds of A4-size documents)
- film is fitted into a viewer to view documents in an enlarged form

Advantages of Microfilming
- reduces the space taken up by filing paper documents in vertical and lateral filing cabinets (saving in floor space and filing cabinets)
- film more durable (longer-lasting) than paper
- film is less expensive to send by mail
- copies can easily be made from film
- less risk of losing records

Microfilm Equipment
- reader (viewer) – used for reading microfilm
- camera – for filming documents
- processor – used by organisations to develop their own film

3c   Storage and Retrieval of Information: Security of Information

Why do organisations use passwords?

Passwords are used to prevent unauthorised access to computer files. Passwords are made up of letters, numbers or a combination of both. Often passwords are used along with user identification (ID). The computer operator has to key in her/his own ID and then key in her/his own password before files can be opened and data accessed.

> **Password** = a code made up of letters, numbers or a combination of both which must be entered on a computer system before files can be opened and data accessed

DO	DON'T
• change your password regularly • use a mixture of upper- and lower-case characters • use a combination of letters and numbers or unusual spellings of words • memorise your password • keep your password confidential	• write your password on a post-it and stick it on to your VDU • write your password on a piece of paper and put it in the drawer of your workstation or write it in your diary • use real words • use your own name, names of relatives, birthdays or house numbers as passwords – these may be easily guessed or worked out • tell anyone else your password

How should floppy disks be handled and stored?

DO	DON'T
• label all disks accurately • write on disk labels before attaching them to disks • store disks upright in disk boxes • use disk travel pouches/boxes when transporting disks • keep disks in dust jackets when disks are not being used • slide disks gently into the floppy disk drive, holding the disk by the label and with the label side up • store floppy disks in lockable disk boxes when not in use (disk boxes should be stored in lockable cupboards at the end of the day)	• stick one disk label on top of another • pack disks tightly together • place rubber bands around disks • place heavy objects on top of disks • force disks into the disk drive • remove disks from the disk drive when its light is on • place disks near a magnetic source (including on top of the processor or monitor) • expose disks to strong sunlight or high temperatures

What methods do organisations use to keep ICT software and data secure?

- passwords
- security/ID cards and keys – these need to be inserted into the computer to gain access to the system
- other security devices – voiceprint, fingerprint, iris ('eye') or signature scanners may be used to control access to systems

An organisation may decide to restrict access to particular folders or files on a 'need to know' basis, eg the entry of a wages assistant's user ID may allow access to wages files only. In some organisations, employees may be required to make a written request before being able to access certain files – the request will have to state why the employee wishes access to the files and may require to be authorised by the employee's line manager.

What is a computer virus?

A computer virus is a program which has been created to interfere with computer systems. The virus may result in a message (supposedly funny) being displayed on screen, the system failing or hard drives being wiped of information. Viruses can spread from one computer to another by copying themselves on to disks – when the infected disk is used in another computer, it will transfer the virus to the other computer system. Viruses are often spread through infected e-mail – when the infected e-mail is opened the virus is transferred on to the computer system. Viruses can be very damaging and costly to organisations. It is, therefore, important for organisations to protect their computer systems by installing effective anti-virus software. The anti-virus software can be set to automatically scan and clean ('disinfect') both the computer system and any disk placed in the computer. Organisations must ensure that anti-virus software is updated on a regular basis.

What should a computer operator do if she/he has to leave a workstation (even for a short time)?

- activate a password-protected screensaver or carry out 'save and shut down' procedures – this avoids sensitive information being left on screen
- remove any working disk from the disk drive
- write-protect the disk (eg by moving the tab at the bottom of a floppy disk) to protect the contents
- store the disk in a lockable disk box (the disk box should be stored in a cupboard – preferably in a separate room)

Where employees use computers in areas which are open to the public they should make sure that computer screens are positioned so that they cannot be read by visitors.

Printouts should not be left lying around workstations for other people to read.

What is meant by 'back up procedures'?

Computer data should be copied (backed up) regularly as data held on a computer disk may be lost or corrupted due to:
- computer system faults – resulting in programs failing
- fire, flood or computer virus
- malicious damage to hardware or software
- theft of the computer and/or disks
- power to the computer being accidentally interrupted or disconnected.

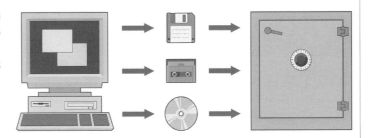

An organisation should have procedures for backing up important data on a regular basis. Whenever a large amount of information has been keyed in or updated, a copy should be made – information should be backed up on to a separate disk or on to tape. In large organisations, backing up may be done automatically overnight.

The back up copy should be stored separately from the disk on which the original (master) file is kept – preferably in a locked fireproof cabinet in a different building. If something happens to the master file then the back up copy can be used.

Back up disks should not be kept near the computer – a thief is likely to steal the disks along with the computer system.

What are the main provisions of the Data Protection Acts (1984 and 1998)?

The Data Protection Act (1984) was introduced because of concerns about personal privacy following rapid growth in the amount of data being held on computer systems.

The Data Protection Acts provide rights for individuals and require organisations to follow good information-handling practice. The 1984 Act covers information stored on computer systems – it does not cover manual records, ie information held in paper files.

(The Data Protection Act 1998 sets a standard for data protection throughout all countries of the European Union. The 1998 Act applies to some manual as well as computerised information, eg health records, school records, and some social services and housing records.)

Anyone (apart from a few limited exceptions) who holds information about living individuals on a computer must be registered as a **data user** with the **Data Protection Registrar**. Following registration, data users must comply with the **Data Protection Principles**. The Principles state that **personal data** must be:
- collected and processed fairly and lawfully
- held only for the specified and lawful purposes described in the register
- used only for the purposes described in the register and disclosed only to those people described in the register
- adequate, relevant and not excessive
- accurate and kept up to date
- held for no longer than necessary
- protected by proper security.

The Principles also state that individuals must be able to access the data held about themselves and, where appropriate, have it corrected or erased.

> **Data User** = almost anyone who controls and uses a collection of personal data held on computer
>
> **Personal Data** = information about a living, identifiable person

Where a data user does not comply with the Principles, the Registrar can serve three types of notice:
- an enforcement notice (the data user is required to take specified action to comply with the particular Principle)
- a deregistration notice (cancels the whole or part of a data user's register entry)
- a transfer prohibition notice (prevents the data user from transferring personal data overseas).

Failure to comply with any of the above notices is a criminal offence.

4 Reprographics

What are the features and uses of reprographics equipment?

Equipment	Features	Uses
Photocopier	• an exact copy of the document is produced • used to produce single or multiple copies of documents • on some photocopiers, copies can also be made on to A5- or A3-size paper • most photocopying uses powdered ink (toner) • most copiers can be set to reduce, enlarge, lighten or darken • some photocopiers can automatically feed in multi-page documents • some copiers can collate (collect copied pages of multi-page documents in order) and staple documents • colour copiers are also available • some modern photocopiers can also print directly from a computer, ie no paper original is required	• wide range of documents, including printed text, charts, handwritten documents and graphics, can be copied • copies can be made on to paper, thin card or OHP transparencies
Laminator	• coats paper or thin card with a clear plastic seal • paper/card is protected – dirty marks can be easily wiped off • useful where a piece of paper/card is likely to be handled many times	• identity cards • instruction sheets • notices

Binder	• fastens multi-page documents together
	• improves the appearance of the document
	• with a **spiral comb binder**, holes are punched down the left edge of the document and a plastic spine fitted through the holes – the spine may be removed and individual pages taken out or copied as necessary
	• with a **flat comb binder**, two plastic strips are placed on either side of the document and heat-sealed (thermal bound) to keep the pages together
		• used where related papers are too thick to be stapled
		• may also be used to improve the appearance of:
		  • reports
		  • instruction booklets
		  • plans

Scanner	• scans source material (drawings, photographs, printed text, etc) and saves it as a computer file for storage, manipulation or insertion into other documents • with a **flatbed scanner** the source material is placed on to a glass plate and a light-sensitive scanning device moves across the image and converts it into digital form	• to scan line drawings, photographs, text, etc, for insertion into other documents
DTP software	• documents are prepared using a DTP application, eg Adobe PageMaker or Microsoft Publisher • text, graphics, photographs, etc can be combined, manipulated and laid out on screen • allows production of high-quality documents	• magazines • newsletters • price lists • posters • forms • manuals • leaflets • booklets, eg on health and safety • catalogues

5 Sources of Information

What type of information do organisations require?

- train/air/ferry services and times
- weather forecasts
- road conditions
- hotels
- garages
- services, eg courier, office supplies, printing agency, service engineer and taxi
- foreign exchange rates
- spelling and meaning of words
- phone and fax numbers
- Royal Mail postal services

It is impossible for an office worker to carry in her/his head all the information likely to be required by an organisation – what is important is that the office worker knows where to find the information required.

What sources of information are used by organisations?

- people (face-to-face conversations, meetings, phone conversations, etc)
- paper-based sources (books, directories, newspapers, brochures, leaflets, manuals, catalogues, lists, records, files, etc)
- ICT-based sources, eg TV (teletext) and computer (computer files, e-mail, electronic diary, CD-ROM, remote databases, intranet and the Internet)

Examples of Paper-Based Sources of Information
- *Whitaker's Almanack*
- *Pears Cyclopaedia*
- *Roget's Thesaurus*
- *Who's Who*
- *Atlas of the World*
- *The Phone Book*
- *Chambers Dictionary*

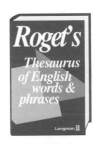

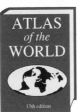

What sources of information are used by organisations? (cont.)

ICT-based Sources of Information

TV – Teletext (Ceefax, 5 text, etc)

- news
- finance
- TV guides
- entertainment
- share prices
- weather
- road conditions
- sports news
- foreign exchange rates
- train and air services

Computer

- computer files (word-processed, spreadsheet and database documents and records – possibly accessed through an intranet)
- e-mail
- electronic diary (times and dates of meetings and appointments, names and addresses of customers, phone and fax numbers, e-mail addresses, priorities lists, etc)
- internal databases (databases set up and updated by the organisation) including lists of suppliers and customers
- remote databases (databases set up by other organisations)
  - accessed through the Internet
  - available to specialist groups (closed user groups) only, eg holiday and airline seat information available to travel agents or prices of shares available to financial institutions

What is an intranet?

- an intranet is a form of internal computer network – information on an intranet is usually available only to the organisation's employees
- an intranet allows an organisation's employees to share software applications and data
- the intranet server stores all the software applications and data – workstations are connected to the server

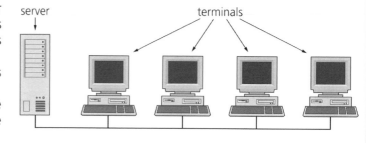

- access to the organisation's intranet is controlled by the organisation
- most intranets use the same technologies as the Internet – data is likely to be displayed in the format of web pages
- employees can create pages of information, eg employees' phone numbers, to be viewed by other employees
- an organisation can set up connections to allow employees to access the Internet from the intranet

Advantages	Disadvantages
• employees are provided with fast and easy access to the same, up-to-date information from any of the organisation's workstations	• staff require training to set up pages and to use the intranet
• should reduce costs of reproducing and circulating information, eg the internal phone directory can be placed on the intranet, eliminating the need to issue paper copies to all employees	• computer network may be costly to set up
• reduced software applications costs	• if the network breaks down, staff may be unable to access software applications or data
• the same versions of applications are accessed from the intranet server	

Uses

- any frequently-consulted document (eg price lists, newsletters, customer/supplier lists, organisational policies/procedures, internal job vacancies, staff handbooks and annual reports) can be placed on the intranet
- newsgroups can be set up which allow groups of employees to exchange information
- a site can be set up to display answers to 'Frequently Asked Questions' (FAQs)

What information is available on CD-ROM?

The following are just a few examples of the types of information available on CD-ROM:

- *Business Abstracts*
- census information
- *Regional Trends*
- *Social Trends*
- road maps and routes
- back issues of newspapers (eg *The Times*, the *Financial Times*, the *Herald*, *The Scotsman* and *Scotland on Sunday*)
- magazines and journals (eg *British Medical Journal* and *The Economist*)
- *Encyclopaedia Britannica*
- *Who's Who*.

What is the Internet?

The Internet is an open-access worldwide communications network which links vast numbers of computers and computer networks. The computer networks which make up the Internet are operated by governments, universities, colleges and increasingly by commercial organisations.

What do you need to access the Internet?

- computer
- modem (internal or external) to connect the computer to the phone network
- a phone line
- an account with an Internet Service Provider (ISP)
- communications software

Some large organisations have direct access to the Internet. Most people, however, access the Internet through an ISP such as CompuServe, Demon or AOL.

ISPs usually have connection points in large towns and cities which provide access to the Internet at local phone call rates.

There are many service deals available from ISPs. At the time of writing, a number of ISPs were discontinuing connection time charges in exchange for a one-off connection fee and a small annual charge.

What services are available on the Internet?

- e-mail
- newsgroups – allow users who have common special interests or hobbies to 'talk' to each other and share information
- World Wide Web (www) – gives users access to well over 500 million pages of information (a collection of related web pages is known as a **website**); the World Wide Web is increasingly being used for **electronic commerce** (**e-commerce**) – the sale and purchase of goods and services on the Internet
- ftp (file transfer protocol) – allows users to send files (text, programs, graphics, etc) to one another (many ftp files will be compressed ['zipped'] so as to take up less disk space – the user has to have the necessary software to decompress ['unzip'] such files)

How do you find information on the World Wide Web?

Search engines (eg those provided by Yahoo, AltaVista, Lycos and Excite) help users to locate information. Most search engines are free. Search engines look through the opening words of each website and create an index of sites. This index is then matched with the search word(s) keyed in by the user.

Web pages often contain **hyperlinks** (hotspots – highlighted words or images) to other web pages. By clicking on a hyperlink the user can jump to another page on the same website or to a different website.

Web page addresses are known as **URLs** (Uniform Resource Locators). URL is a standard naming convention which helps users to navigate the World Wide Web. Each web page has a unique URL.

Most web page addresses have a common structure:

http://www.made4it.co.uk

hypertext transfer protocol — world wide web — name of organisation — type of organisation — country

E-mail addresses follow a similar structure (except for 'http://www'), eg **sam.ryan@made4it.co.uk**

Some e-mail addresses include the name of the ISP.

Users must be very careful with e-mail addresses – for example, an e-mail will not reach the intended destination if in the address an upper-case letter is keyed in by mistake instead of a lower-case letter.

Computer files (word-processed documents, spreadsheets, graphics, etc) can be sent as **attachments** to e-mail messages. The attached file is an exact copy of the original and can be printed or edited as required.

Confidential or sensitive information should be **encrypted** before being sent over the Internet. Encryption software puts the message into code – if the message is intercepted it cannot be read. The recipient must, of course, have the necessary software and password/key to decode the message.

The **Home Page** is the first web page which a user sees when she/he accesses the World Wide Web. A user can choose any web page as her/his Home Page.

Web browser software (eg Netscape Communicator or Microsoft Internet Explorer) is used to access the World Wide Web.

The '**Bookmarks**' (or '**Favorites**') facility allows users to save the addresses of web pages which they are likely to visit frequently. Instead of keying in a long web page address each time, the user simply has to click on the saved address.

What information is available on the Internet?

The following are just a few examples of the vast range of information available through the Internet:
- travel (eg ScotRail, Scottish Citylink, London Transport, Eurostar, Caledonian MacBrayne, Streetmaps [UK])
- hotels (eg Jarvis, Holiday Inn, Forte, Posthouse, Stakis)
- weather (eg World Climate, World Weather)
- companies (eg Companies Online)
- English language (eg *Roget's Thesaurus*, *Webster's Dictionary*)
- media (newspapers, eg the *Daily Telegraph*, the *Guardian*, the *Observer*, *The Times*; broadcasting, eg BBC and Channel 4; magazines, eg *The Economist*, *New Scientist*, *National Geographic*, *Time*)
- government (eg Central Office of Information, Department of Health, Inland Revenue, Department of the Environment, Transport and the Regions, Home Office, Health and Safety Executive, Foreign Office, Her Majesty's Treasury, Data Protection Registrar)
- political parties
- general (eg *Britannica Online*)
- Yellow Pages.

It should be noted that not all of the above provide free access.

There are certain websites, such as http://www.ukonline.gov.uk, which provide links to related sites. This can save a great deal of time in tracking down a piece of information.

How does an organisation create its own website?

1 rents space on an ISP's host computer
2 designs the web pages which are to make up the website (or employs a specialist firm to do this)
3 places the pages on the ISP's host computer
4 advertises the existence of the website (on letterhead, business cards, mailshots, etc)

How do you use a browser and search engine?

In the picture below it can be seen that the browser Microsoft Internet Explorer has been used to access Yahoo's search engine. (Remember that web pages are always being updated – if you accessed Yahoo today it would look slightly different.)

toolbar (see below for more details)

web address for Yahoo

key in word(s) to search for here, then click on 'Search'

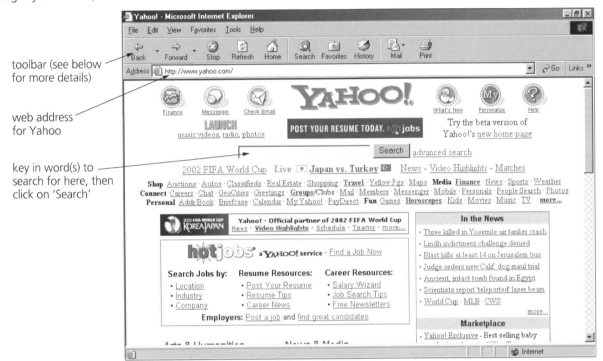

The following table shows what happens when toolbar buttons are clicked.

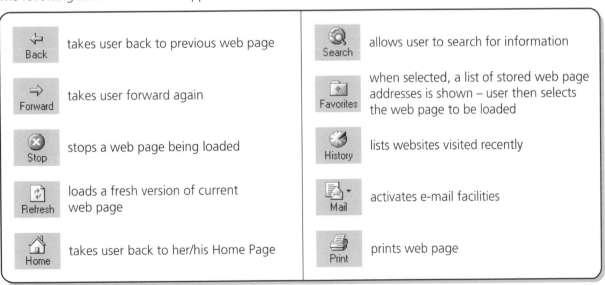

Back takes user back to previous web page	**Search** allows user to search for information
Forward takes user forward again	**Favorites** when selected, a list of stored web page addresses is shown – user then selects the web page to be loaded
Stop stops a web page being loaded	**History** lists websites visited recently
Refresh loads a fresh version of current web page	**Mail** activates e-mail facilities
Home takes user back to her/his Home Page	**Print** prints web page

6 Preparation and Presentation of Information

How is information prepared and presented?

An organisation will often need to prepare and present facts and figures to show how well it is performing compared with previous years or compared with the performance of similar organisations.

People usually find facts and figures easier to understand if they are shown graphically, eg in the form of line graphs and charts.

Graphs and charts can be prepared directly from data using a variety of software, including spreadsheet and word processing applications.

Form	Features	When used
Line Graph SALES FOR 2000	• single- or multi-line • requires a title • each axis should be labelled • scale should be shown on the vertical axis • points are joined together by straight lines • lines can be shown in different colours or as continuous and broken lines • codes should be shown in a key • where appropriate, the source of the data should be stated	• useful for showing comparisons and trends over short periods of time, eg figures for sales, purchases, profits and prices • allows for detailed comparisons to be made
Pictogram CAR PRODUCTION FOR 2000	• use of pictures or symbols to represent statistical information (eg a car to represent 10,000 cars or a bottle of milk to represent 100,000 bottles of milk) • must have a key to the use of symbols • simple and eye-catching	• used to show statistical information when precise and detailed figures are not required • used to provide a quick, general impression
Bar Chart SALES OF PRINTERS	• bars may be shown vertically or horizontally • similar in layout to line graph • different colours can be used to distinguish different bars • bars should be of equal width • eye-catching • another form is a segmented/stacked bar chart	• useful for showing and contrasting figures for short periods of time • can show more detailed information than a pie chart
Pie Chart ADMINISTRATION COURSE CONTENT	• circle represents total amount, ie 100% • eye-catching • segments of circle show proportion of whole • the percentage represented by each segment should be shown • segments may be shown in different colours	• useful for broad comparisons (pie charts do not show detailed information)

Form	Features	When used
Flow Chart  **'GOING TO WORK' PROCEDURE** 	• starting and finishing points shown in rounded boxes • a step or action is shown in a rectangular box • arrows between the boxes show which box (step) to move on to • a decision or question is shown in a diamond-shaped box	• useful for showing or explaining the steps in a system or procedure • useful where it is important that staff go through each step in a complex procedure
Itinerary 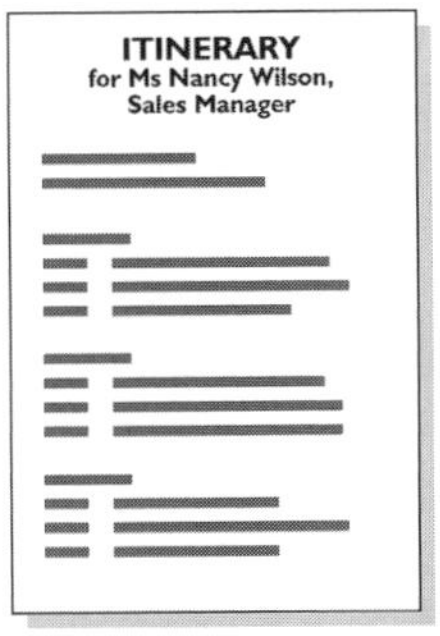 **ITINERARY** **for Ms Nancy Wilson, Sales Manager** 	• who is going on trip ⎫ • where trip is to ⎬ Heading • date(s) of trip ⎭ • details of the trip are listed in date order • details include: • modes of travel • times of travel • place of departure and arrival, eg name of airport • reservations, eg seats and accommodation • appointments (See page 76 for example of layout.)	• when a member of staff is going on a business trip • assists the member of staff by providing information on travel arrangements and appointments
Memorandum (Memo)  **MEMORANDUM** 	• can be on A4- or A5-size paper • no address (sender and receiver work for the same organisation) • not signed • not put into an envelope unless private, personal or confidential • does not include a salutation (eg 'Dear Sir') or a complimentary close (eg 'Yours faithfully')	• form of internal communication • to send a written (handwritten or keyed-in) message between people who work for the same organisation

Layout of Memorandum

- TO: who memo is to
- FROM: who memo is from
- REF: usually the initials of the person who wrote the memo followed by the initials of the person who keyed it in
- DATE: date memo was prepared
- SUBJECT: what memo is about
- MESSAGE – shown below the headings

MEMORANDUM

TO: All Safety Representatives

FROM: Steven Lewis, Health and Safety Manager

REF: SL/RT

DATE: 15 May 2000

SUBJECT: SAFETY COMMITTEE MEETING

Please note that the next meeting of the Safety Committee will be held in my office on Tuesday, 6 June 2000 at 0930 hours.

Reports

There are two main types of report: informal report and formal report

- **informal report**

Features	Layout	When used
• often in the form of a memorandum • usually written in the first person • usually short	• introduction – what the report is about • description of how the information was collected • summary of the information collected • conclusions • recommendations	• when reporting to line manager

- **formal report**

Features	Layout	When used
• written in a formal tone • should be easy to read • tables of facts and figures should be shown in appendices • organisation may have a house style with standard headings and layout	• heading – the title of the report • introduction – the terms of reference section describes the scope and purpose of the report • executive summary (optional) – a summary of the report, usually on one page • procedure – states the main sources of information and the methods used to collect the information • findings – describes what has been found out • conclusions – summarises what can be concluded from the findings • recommendations – proposals, usually numbered, as to the suggested way forward • bibliography – a list of any other publications referred to • appendices • signature and date (See layout of formal report on page 73.)	• to present information on a particular topic (often after research has been carried out) • report may be for consideration by senior management within the organisation • report may also be sent outwith the organisation

Report on the Opportunities for Advertising and Selling on the Internet

1 Terms of Reference

Following recent growth in the use of the World Wide Web for marketing and the rapid rise in the level of e-commerce transactions, the Sales Manager requested the Sales Supervisor to prepare a report on the opportunities for advertising and/or selling Made4IT's products and services over the Internet.

2 Procedure

2.1 A survey was undertaken to establish the number of current customers who use the Internet on a regular basis.

2.2 A meeting was held with Saunders and Kievel, computer analysts, to determine:
- a minimum specification for a website
- costs of setting up a website
- annual running costs of a website
- costs of developing and establishing a website for e-commerce.

3 Findings

3.1 A circular letter was issued to all customers to establish the level of Internet use and the likely level of uptake should Made4IT establish a website to provide information on its products and services. The main findings were as follows:
- 74% of customers used the Internet on a regular basis
- 65% of customers anticipated that they would use the Internet to find out up-to-date information on Made4IT's products/services.

A detailed analysis of the responses is provided in Appendix 1.

3.2 Saunders and Kievel suggested the following minimum specification and costs:
- website to consist of animated home page with hotlinks to six pages of information
- costs of setting up a website (designing, registration, etc) – £1,400
- annual running costs (rental, costs of updating, etc) – £500
- costs of developing a website for e-commerce – £14,500.

Further information is given in Appendix 2.

4 Conclusions

4.1 The level of visits to a website amongst present customers is likely to be high.

4.2 The costs of developing and running a website for advertising purposes are not excessive.

4.3 The costs of developing the website for e-commerce are considerable.

5 Recommendations

5.1 Proceed with the development of a website for advertising purposes only.

5.2 Publicise the website by inclusion of website address in all external communications.

5.3 Review the development of a website for e-commerce in light of the number of visits to Made4IT's website in the first year of operation.

Karen Law

Sales Supervisor

19 May 2000

7a Travel: Arrangements

What arrangements need to be made for a business trip?

A member of staff who is about to leave on a business trip should have:
- a note of all travel and accommodation arrangements and the time and place of all appointments
- all necessary paperwork (including business documents for meetings)
- all transport tickets and reservations
- confirmation of booked accommodation.

How is information gathered for business trips?

To make the most suitable travel and accommodation arrangements, the following information must first be obtained:
- the name and position of the person going on the trip
- the start and finish dates of the trip
- the destination (where the person is going to)
- the purpose of the trip
- places to be visited during the trip
- any preferred method of travel
- any special requirements, eg vegetarian meals, non-smoking travel/accommodation or wheelchair access
- the budget for the trip.

The organisation may require an employee to provide information by completing a standard form (see example Travel/Accommodation Request Form on page 77).

How is the method of travel chosen?

The method of travel chosen (road, rail, air or sea) will depend upon:
- the destination
- the distance to be travelled
- the time available (to reach the destination and for travelling between appointments)
- the policy of the organisation
- whether bulky materials have to be taken on the trip
- the budget for the trip.

What sources of information are used when arranging travel and accommodation?

- timetables, eg British Midland and ScotRail timetables
- travel guides
- hotel chain guides, eg Travel Lodges and Holiday Inns
- directories, eg *The Which? Hotel Guide 2001* and *RAC Inspected Hotels*
- maps
- AA/RAC handbooks
- a list of preferred hotels or hotels used previously by the organisation (the organisation being visited may also suggest suitable local accommodation)

What sources of information are used when arranging travel and accommodation? (cont.)

Information can be obtained from:
- paper-based documents
- travel agents (they may be able to offer better rates on travel and accommodation)
- CD-ROMs
- the Internet (some travel organisations and hotels offer a direct booking service over the Internet).

Using the Internet or the services of a travel agent should save time in gathering together all the necessary information – it should also ensure that the information is up to date. The person making the arrangements must ensure that the organisation's policy, eg on the use of a particular airline, hotel chain or travel agent, is adhered to.

What special arrangements may have to be made for travellers?

Countries may require travellers to have particular documentation or may recommend that travellers have been immunised against certain diseases. The person making the travel arrangements must find out what is required and check that the member of staff has the necessary documentation and has had the necessary immunisations.

A free Department of Health leaflet *Health Advice for Travellers* provides information on health risks, immunisation requirements, how to get treatment around the world, etc.

Documentation	Details
Passport	valid 10-year passport required for travel outwith the UK
Form E111	entitles travellers from the UK to free or reduced-cost emergency medical treatment in European Union countries (also applies to some other European countries)
Visa	check whether a visa is required for any country being visited outwith Europe
Immunisation Form	check for any immunisation requirements (eg against hepatitis A, typhoid, yellow fever, tetanus, meningitis, polio and tuberculosis) for countries being visited outwith Europe

Other items which may be required:
- UK/International driving licence
- car hire information
- first-aid kit (containing adhesive dressings, insect repellent, antiseptic cream, water-sterilisation tablets, etc)
- personal insurance, health insurance, travel insurance
- credit/debit cards
- phone chargecard
- maps
- names, addresses and phone numbers of organisations to be visited.

What travel documents require to be completed?

Itinerary
An itinerary is a working document which provides key information on travel, accommodation and appointments in order of date and time.

Points to consider when preparing an itinerary:
- avoid making the schedule too tight – do not attempt to cram in appointments
- allow time for the traveller to relax, especially after a long trip
- take account of international time zones and the possible effects on the traveller
- use the 24-hour clock; show times as local times
- provide information on check-in times
- allow time for any necessary travel between stations and airport terminals

- **who** is travelling

- **where** they are travelling to
- **start** and **finish dates** of travel

- **modes of travel**, eg air, road

- **times of travel**, eg check-in, departure, arrival, any air terminal or rail station changes

- **locations**, eg name of airport or rail station, air terminal, flight numbers

- **reservations**, eg name, address and phone number of accommodation; seat reservations, sleeping berths

- **appointments**, eg time, name of contact, address, phone number

ITINERARY for Ms Nancy Wilson, Sales Manager

Aberdeen and Amsterdam
Monday 15 to Wednesday 17 May 2000

Monday 15 May

0730 hours	Taxi (booked) from home to Perth rail station.
0842 hours	Train departs Perth (ticket for 1st class travel).
1021 hours	Train arrives Aberdeen rail station.
	Take taxi (outside rail station) to appointment.
1100 hours	Meeting at Dean Office Services, 23 George Street (tel: 01224 423611) with Mr Ryan Spence, Purchasing Manager. File No 342 has the information for the meeting.
	Lunch arranged by Dean Office Services.
1440 hours	Dean Office Services has arranged for their car to take you to Aberdeen Airport.
1520 hours	Check in. Flying BA, Flight No BA1313 to London Heathrow.
1620 hours	Flight departs.
1750 hours	Flight arrives London Heathrow Terminal 1.
2040 hours	Flight departs Terminal 4. Flying BA, Flight No BA444 to Amsterdam.
2245 hours	Flight arrives Amsterdam (local time).
	Use airport courtesy phone for car to take you to Waterloo Hotel, Hasselts Straat (tel: 020 623 83 98). Late check in and supper arranged with hotel.

Tuesday 16 May

0930 hours	Exhibition opens at Grand Hotel Martinn, Dam Square. This is within walking distance from hotel (map and information booklet on Amsterdam included). Spend day at exhibition.
1930 hours	Dinner booked at your hotel with M Alain Hartelaub and Mme Stephanie Merlo of Euro Designs.

Wednesday 17 May

	Use hotel courtesy car to go to Airport.
1350 hours	Check in at Departure Hall 1. Flying BA, Flight No BA1627 to Manchester.
1450 hours	Flight departs.
1500 hours	Flight arrives Manchester (local time).
1700 hours	Flight departs. Flying BA, Flight No BA1655 to Edinburgh.
1805 hours	Flight arrives Edinburgh.
	Take airport taxi to Edinburgh Waverley rail station.
	Make own arrangements for train travel from Edinburgh to Perth. Train departure times are 1940 hours, 2015 hours and 2033 hours (train timetable included).

Travel/Accommodation Request Form

TRAVEL/ACCOMMODATION REQUEST FORM

EMPLOYEE DETAILS

Title	Surname	First Name	Department
Mr	*Smith*	*Graham*	*Finance*

REASON FOR BUSINESS TRIP

To gather information on a number of possible sites for a new European warehouse in or near Paris

TRAVEL/ACCOMMODATION DETAILS

Departure Date *10/4/2000* Place of Departure *Edinburgh* Place of Arrival *Paris*

Return Date *12/4/2000* Place of Departure *Paris* Place of Arrival *Edinburgh*

Places to be Visited	Dates of Stay	Accommodation Preferred
PARIS	*10-12/4/2000*	*HOTEL*

Preferred form of travel *AIR*

OTHER REQUIREMENTS

~~Smoking~~/Non-Smoking*   Itinerary Required YES/~~NO~~*

Special Requests *Meeting room in hotel on 11/4/2000*

Visa ~~YES~~/NO*   Vaccinations ~~YES~~/NO*

* Delete as appropriate

Signed *Graham Smith*   Date *14 March 2000*

Travel Booking Form
Once the method of travel has been selected, the person making the arrangements may be required to complete a Travel Booking Form (see example on page 78). This form is sent to whoever is booking the travel, eg the travel agent.

Accommodation Order Form
Once the hotel and type of accommodation have been selected, the person making the arrangements may be required to complete an Accommodation Order Form (see example on page 78). This form is sent to the booking agency or the hotel.

These forms can be referred to should there be any dispute about the travel or accommodation arrangements.

If an organisation does not use forms when booking travel and accommodation, or if travel and accommodation have been booked by phone or over the Internet, then a letter or fax should be sent to confirm the arrangements. A copy of the letter or fax can be referred to should there be any dispute about the arrangements.

**10 Newhouse Avenue
PERTH
PHI2 6XJ**

TRAVEL BOOKING FORM

TO

Star Travel Ltd
1 9 Craig Park
PERTH
PH9 4XJ

NO | 2000/1 2/F/T

Please book the following travel requirements for _Graham Smith_ and send the bill for the attention of _Sam Ryan_ to the above address.

Date	Time	From	To	Details	Cost
10/4/00	0635	Edinburgh Airport	Charles de Gaulle Airport, Paris	Business Class	£220 return
12/4/00	1528	Charles de Gaulle Airport, Paris	Edinburgh Airport	Business Class	

This order for travel has been authorised by:

Signature ...._Sam Ryan_.............................

Designation......._Admin Supervisor_....................... Date ..._29 March 2000_..............

**10 Newhouse Avenue
PERTH
PHI2 6XJ**

ACCOMMODATION ORDER FORM

TO

Hotel Opera
1 9 rue Buffault
PARIS
France

NO | 2000/1 2/F/A

Please book the following requirements for _Graham Smith_ and send the bill for the attention of _Sam Ryan_ to the above address.

Date	Time		Requirements	Details of other facilities requested	Cost
	From	To			
10/4/00	1100		1 single room bed	Small meeting room for 1 1/4/00	£85 per night
12/4/00		0700	and breakfast non-smoking		£40 for meeting room

This order for accommodation has been authorised by:

Signature ...._Sam Ryan_.............................

Designation......._Admin Supervisor_....................... Date ..._29 March 2000_..............

How do people and organisations pay for travel, meals and accommodation?

Payment(s) may need to be made to:
- a travel agent
- a travel operator, eg an airline or ferry operator
- hotel(s)
- restaurant(s)
- a car hire firm.

Various methods of payment can be used, eg cash, account, cheque, credit card or debit card.

Cash
If travelling abroad, local currency should be purchased in advance (from a bank, travel agent, building society, etc) for the traveller to pay for car hire, taxis, refreshments, etc. The traveller should keep an accurate record of cash expenses and obtain receipts of expenditure whenever possible.

Account
An organisation which deals directly with a travel agent, travel operator or hotel may be sent an invoice (bill) for travel and/or accommodation costs.

Cheque
A cheque is likely to be sent or given to the travel agent, travel operator or hotel to settle an invoice.

Credit Card (eg Visa card and MasterCard)
A credit card is used to pay for goods/services on credit (to be paid for at a later date). Credit cards are widely accepted in the UK and in most countries around the world. Paying bills by credit card should reduce the need to carry large amounts of cash. Credit cards are very useful when paying for hotel accommodation and meals in restaurants. Payment by credit card is made by:
- the person being paid 'swiping' the card through a terminal (the person paying then signs a sales voucher and receives a copy of the voucher), or
- quoting the credit card number and expiry date of the card over the phone, or
- keying the credit card number (and other details) in to a computer for an Internet transaction.

A monthly statement is received from the credit card company detailing all the transactions. If the whole amount is paid then no interest is charged – if only part-payment is made then interest is charged on the balance still owing.

Debit Card (eg Switch and Delta)
A debit card can also be used to pay for goods/services.
- the person being paid 'swipes' the card through a terminal (the person paying then signs a sales voucher and receives a copy of the voucher)
- the amount is withdrawn immediately (via a computerised network) from the bank account of the person paying and paid into the bank account of the hotel, shop, restaurant, etc

How do organisations check and verify expenditure?

To pay for expenses whilst on a business trip an organisation may provide a member of staff with:
- a credit card or debit card
- foreign currency, eg euros, dollars or roubles
- travellers' cheques
- a phone chargecard.

In some organisations, members of staff may be required to pay for expenses themselves and reclaim the expenses on return. On return, the member of staff would have to complete an Expenses Claim Form (see example on page 80) and attach to it any receipts for expenses paid. The Expenses Claim Form would then be checked carefully by the organisation to ensure that it was correct before the expenses were paid.

EXPENSES CLAIM FORM

Employees should attach all receipts and invoices. Payment of expenses may be delayed if documentation is missing.

Name _Graham Smith_   Department _Finance_

Dates of travel _10/4/2000 – 12/4/2000_		Total expenditure (including VAT)		Accounts use only	
Reason(s) for claim		£	p	Pass for payment (☒)	Withhold payment: (R) – reason (A) – action to be taken
1. Air travel					
2. Sea travel					
3. Car hire					
4. Mileage (own car) _60_ miles at employee rate	_To and from Edinburgh Airport and home_	18	00		(R) Question mileage (A) Check records
5. Rail travel	_Book of Metro tickets_	5	00	☒	
6. Hotel					
7. Lunch	_10/4/2000_	8	50	☒	
	_11/4/2000_	7	80	☒	
8. Dinner	_10/4/2000_	12	80	☒	
	_11/4/2000_	14	60	☒	
9. Other expenses (please detail)	_Airport parking_	19	80		(R) No receipt (A) Request receipt
Total Expenses Due		86	50		

Employee's Signature _Graham Smith_   Date _14/04/00_   Approved by _____

(Return to Graham Smith for clarification)